PERGAMON INTERNATIONAL LIBRARY
of Science, Technology, Engineering and Social Studies

The 1000-volume original paperback library in aid of education,
industrial training and the enjoyment of leisure

Publisher: Robert Maxwell, M.C.

The Effective Psychotherapist
(PGPS - 105)

THE PERGAMON TEXTBOOK
INSPECTION COPY SERVICE

An inspection copy of any book published in the Pergamon International Library
will gladly be sent to academic staff without obligation for their consideration for
course adoption or recommendation. Copies may be retained for a period of 60 days
from receipt and returned if not suitable. When a particular title is adopted or
recommended for adoption for class use and the recommendation results in a sale
of 12 or more copies the inspection copy may be retained with our compliments.
The Publishers will be pleased to receive suggestions for revised editions and new
titles to be published in this important international Library.

Pergamon Titles of Related Interest

Related Journals*

The Effective Psychotherapist
Conclusions from Practice and Research

David Brenner
Colgate University

PERGAMON PRESS

New York • Oxford • Beijing • Frankfurt
São Paulo • Sydney • Tokyo • Toronto

Pergamon Press Offices:

U.S.A.   Pergamon Press, Maxwell House, Fairview Park,
                Elmsford, New York 10523, U.S.A.

U.K.   Pergamon Press, Headington Hill Hall,
                Oxford OX3 0BW, England

PEOPLE'S REPUBLIC   Pergamon Press, Qianmen Hotel, Beijing,
OF CHINA   People's Republic of China

FEDERAL REPUBLIC   Pergamon Press, Hammerweg 6,
OF GERMANY   D-6242 Kronberg, Federal Republic of Germany

BRAZIL   Pergamon Editora, Rua Eça de Queiros, 346,
                CEP 04011, São Paulo, Brazil

AUSTRALIA   Pergamon Press (Aust.) Pty., P.O. Box 544,
                Potts Point, NSW 2011, Australia

JAPAN   Pergamon Press, 8th Floor, Matsuoka Central Building,
                1-7-1 Nishishinjuku, Shinjuku-ku, Tokyo 160, Japan

CANADA   Pergamon Press Canada, Suite 104, 150 Consumers Road,
                Willowdale, Ontario M2J 1P9, Canada

Copyright © 1982 Pergamon Press Inc.

Second printing 1987

Library of Congress Cataloging in Publication Data

Brenner, David, 1944-
    The effective psychotherapist.

    (Pergamon general psychology series ;
v. 105)
    Bibliography: p.
    Includes index.
    1. Psychotherapy. I. Title. II. Series.
RC480.5.B74   616.89'14   81-13911
ISBN 0-08-028056-0   AACR2
ISBN 0-08-028055-2 (pbk.)

Printed in Great Britain by A. Wheaton & Co., Ltd, Exeter.

For my mother and father

Contents

Foreword   ix

Preface   xiii

Acknowledgments   xv

CHAPTER

  1 The Helping Relationship: Therapist
     Characteristics   1

  2 The First Meeting   14

  3 The Client's Strengths   26

  4 Easily Observable Physical Characteristics:
     Age, Gender, and Skin Color   39

  5 Psychoactive Drugs   56

  6 Crossroads   75

  7 Trust, Privilege, and Confidentiality   87

Coda   103

References   105

Author Index   117

Subject Index   123

About the Author   125

Foreword

Lee Sechrest
University of Michigan

I have always been uncomfortable with the common opposition of art *vs.* science in relation to psychotherapy. Art is intuitive, unconstrained by reason, recalcitrant to demands for practicality and utility. Science is more definite, rational, based in firm knowledge, and, even when theoretical, always in the long run anticipating application. Somehow it seemed to me that psychotherapy surely could not be an art, however exalted, and probably it could never be exactly a science either. Recently it occurred to me while contemplating my experiences in browsing through a huge summer "art" show that the word *craft* is a much better descriptor of the practice of psychotherapy, connoting as it does the amalgam of art and knowledge, imagination and technique. Psychotherapy must on occasion be intuitive, on occasion somewhat magical, but it must also be based more generally on a firm bed of knowledge and expressed in finely honed techniques. What we think of and admire as the products of fine craftsmen are just such a combination. I suspect that an effective psychotherapist is, in truth, a craftsman, bringing to bear both his imagination and his scientific knowledge on the problems at hand; now a bit more of one than the other, but nearly always in a skillful blend.

In my present position I am concerned with the ways in which scientific knowledge gets utilized and the factors that determine utilization. The factors are many. Scientific data can be of uncertain quality or immediate relevance. Factors other than truth may enter, e.g., politics and economics. Sometimes the utilization of a bit of scientific knowledge may be difficult because that utilization would require too many other changes in the system. And often there is simply an all too human lag that makes it easier, and perhaps preferable, to go on doing things in familiar ways rather than to venture into new ones. Finally, despite all evidence of the senses, scientific knowledge may simply be disbelieved by some. So, I am sure, it must be with psychotherapy. In that area of human ameliorative endeavor we ought, however, to be concerned with the relationship between scientific evidence and practice and in ways of ensuring that knowledge, where it exists does become part of the amalgam of the craft and that, where it does not, it at least provides part of the matrix within which art may come into play.

Perhaps I would have entitled David Brenner's book *The Craft of Psychotherapy*, for it is, I believe, a remarkable demonstration of the way in which personal experience and intuition may be interwoven with information obtained from research to produce an integral whole. David—and my long personal acquaintance with him precludes greater formality—does an excellent job of bringing to bear scientific information where it exists and at the same time making sure that personal experience and intuition do not, when they are cited, violate the reason provided by science. His treatise has integrity in the same sense that a fine piece of craftsmanship expresses the essence of material in a balanced blend of imagination and technique. I have read works on psychotherapy that at one point invoke scientific findings in favor of one approach to a problem and at another point recommend an entirely different intuitive strategy. David avoids that, probably unthinking, duplicity. Science, experience, and plain good sense are carefully blended in views and recommendations that are of a piece.

As is clear, this book is to a considerable extent a personal statement, and a potential reader may legitimately inquire about what it is that makes this statement worth reading. The statement should have the same legitimacy as the inquiry. Training is the beginning of the answer, I think—perhaps understandably since I helped to train David. But he came of age as a clinical psychologist at Northwestern University at a time when it was noted, we thought preeminent, for its strong commitment to empirical data obtained by the best research methods. Imagination was prized in developing theory but not in developing facts. Second, it seems to me that David has had a good bit of experience, but more than that, he has reflected on that experience with uncommon care. My own mentor, George A. Kelly, used to speak of a man who had 13 years of experience, one year repeated 13 times. My own reading of this book indicates that David has received the full benefits of his experience because of what he has made of it. Finally, David has good communication skills and his writing is for the most part persuasive, and where it is not persuasive it arouses the kinds of personal reflections that are themselves informative. Undoubtedly many readers will have honest disagreements with positions taken in the book, but those disagreements are likely to be experienced as positive challenges. There is craft in writing too.

A wide variety of professionals involved in therapeutic enterprises should benefit from David's book. It will, however, probably have its greatest value for graduate students and those in the early stages of establishing themselves as practitioners. The book is addressed to a variety of practical concerns of consequence, all of which have to be resolved in one way or another. Probably nearly all experienced therapists will have reached their own resolutions of the issues raised, although they might profit considerably from a chance to review them in the light of the thinking of another experienced, thoughtful clinician. Those readers with less experience, including apprentices in the profession, should benefit greatly from the discussions of these issues of practice that will provide a context within which they can work out their own resolutions. The arguments are careful and firm, not dogmatic. Readers of almost any theoretical persuasion should find much of value in this book.

The central issue, after all, is how to further the therapeutic clinical enterprise in such a way that high quality services can be assured. The ameliorative professions have the obligations to deliver the very best services possible, and there is no role in that obligation for vacuous assumptions or complacency. Those of us in the field need to be committed to the responsible practice of psychology, of our craft, and that is what David Brenner's book is all about.

Preface

This book is written for psychotherapists and counselors who wish to become more effective in their work. The principles discussed should be of use to both beginning students and experienced workers who wish to step back for a moment to reexamine their assumptions and procedures.

In chapter 1, five characteristics necessary for effective helping are identified. This chapter, as all of the others, includes actual examples from therapy sessions to clarify the points being made. In addition, each chapter contains support for these points which has been obtained from a broad range of classic and recently published work of colleagues from both "pure" and "applied" settings.

The point is made in chapter 1 that certain characteristics are necessary but not sufficient for effective helping. Chapters 2 through 7 describe events and principles that counselors and therapists need to understand and apply in their work if they are to be consistently effective. Paradoxically, the importance of these issues has been overlooked because they are inseparable from the helping process; and, consequently, their effect on that process has been difficult to clarify.

As implied above, the work of a broad range of professionals—attorneys, psychologists, psychiatrists and other physicians, pastoral counselors, and social workers—has been reviewed in the preparation of this book and is an essential feature of it. Indeed, some of the works that have had a significant impact on me were written by individuals outside of the helping professions (e.g., Norman Cousins' *Anatomy of an illness as perceived by the patient*). The identification of the seven necessary ingredients in an effective helping relationship would not have emerged without such a review.

It may be helpful to say a word about what this book is not. It is not a presentation of yet another new approach to counseling and psychotherapy —that is the last thing we need. It is not a "how to" book. In all likelihood, you already have read more than your share of "cookbooks," which emphasize technique and method at the expense of compassion, sensitivity, and perspective.

It is my hope that you will learn as much from reading this book as I did from writing it. If you do, you will more likely be of help to those who come to you in moments of need.

Acknowledgments

This book would not have been written without the assistance, encouragement, and support of a number of individuals at Colgate University. First, I want to thank those who went out of their way to see to it that I was granted a leave from Colgate to write this book. Second, a grant from the Colgate University Research Council helped in the preparation of the manuscript. Third, I am very grateful for the help I received from the staff of the Colgate library, especially Carolyn Dearnaley.

Three psychologists have been particularly helpful to me in my efforts to improve as a therapist. I want to thank Dr. Joanne Powers, my first therapy supervisor, whose patience, professionalism, and confidence in me meant a very great deal to me. And I want to thank Dr. Paul Dingman, whose exceptional talents as a highly insightful, readily available consultant during our years together at Colgate accelerated my development as a therapist. Finally, I wish to mention Dr. Linden Summers, whose friendship has been invaluable to me.

I am grateful to both Emily Van Vleet, my research assistant, whose hard work at the earliest stages of this book helped me believe that, some day, it might be completed, and to Pat Ryan, whose typing of the manuscript was extremely accurate, reliable, and professional.

I want to thank my wife, Peggy, for her many helpful comments about the manuscript and who, along with our son, Keith, inspired me to do the best job I could.

Last but not least, I want to thank the many clients who trusted me with their feelings; without them, this book could not have been written.

The Effective Psychotherapist

Chapter 1
The Helping Relationship: Therapist Characteristics

In ev'ry age and clime we see
Two of a trade can never agree.
—John Gay,
The rat-catcher and cats

Therapists have discovered that their
practices are more alike than their
theories.
—Ruesch, 1956

This chapter presents a broad range of evidence for three important assumptions. First, there are identifiable therapist characteristics that are, to say the least, highly desirable. Numerous writers (e.g., Haley, 1969; Shertzer & Stone, 1980; Tolbert, 1978) have reached this conclusion and have presented remarkably similar descriptions of these characteristics. In light of current knowledge, it is safe to conclude that these traits, which are reviewed in this chapter, are necessary for successful therapeutic outcome.

Second, your *particular* theoretical orientation and corresponding techniques are not related crucially to therapeutic outcome. Although it is necessary to have a theoretical orientation, at this point, it seems clear that most attempts to define "the best" therapeutic approach and techniques have resulted in large part from misdirected competition among clinicians and among professional groups. Both research and theoretical writing have shifted in recent years toward attempts to identify a general set of desired therapist characteristics—regardless of theoretical orientation. To our credit, we have outgrown asking questions such as, "Which is better, existential therapy, behavioristic, Rogerian, or psychoanalytic?" We know that, regardless of your approach, if you do not bring certain qualities to the helping relationship, you will not rise above mediocrity in your work.

Third, and perhaps most importantly, it is now clear that, although these traits are *necessary*, they are not *sufficient*. The remaining chapters define and discuss six additional components that enter into every therapeutic relationship. Paradoxically, their significance has been underemphasized *because* they are inseparable from therapeutic process and thus difficult to isolate.

If you have the qualities discussed below, your recognition and handling of the six remaining ingredients usually will make the difference between therapeutic success and failure.

Throughout this book, the words "therapist" and "counselor" are used interchangeably; the same is true for the words "therapy" and "counseling." As implied above, attempts to distinguish between these terms have helped neither us nor the clients we see. Others have reached this conclusion. For example, Tolbert (1978), after attempting to distinguish between the two, concluded:

> Many writers use the terms synonymously, and it is quite true that quite often the psychiatrist is offering short-term help to relatively normal individuals and the counselor is providing a therapeutic experience for the counselee. Moreover, counselors draw on approaches and techniques from psychotherapy in working with counselees [p. 132].

It is my belief that—regardless of your professional discipline and training, regardless of your theoretical orientation, regardless of your customary methods and techniques—you will find the following description of necessary helper characteristics beneficial.

EMPATHY

To be helped, a client must be understood. Further, this understanding must be communicated. A client must know that you are listening carefully and that you understand his or her unique feelings and circumstances. "Empathy" is this ability to see and experience the world as someone else does—to put yourself in another's shoes. Indeed, some believe that this process is the heart and definition of therapy. Bruch (1974) describes psychotherapy as "a situation where two people interact and try to come to an understanding of one another, with the specific goal of accomplishing something beneficial for the complaining person [p. ix]." Strupp (1978) has concluded that empathic understanding must be present to promote therapeutic learning, and Tolbert (1978) similarly has stated that empathic ability is a *sine qua non* for effective counselors.

Increasingly, controlled laboratory studies have operationalized and clarified the significance of empathic ability. For example, Kepics (1979) found that therapists who do not listen adequately lead clients "off the track" and unintentionally elicit client opposition, blocking, and self-criticism. Kepics found that therapists can be taught to recognize these "tracking errors" and to decrease their frequency. In Kepics' study, client opposition, blocking, and self-criticism decreased in proportion to the increase in the counselor's demonstration of empathy.

You cannot overestimate the value of careful listening and your struggle to see the world through a client's eyes. At times, at the end of the first visit or at the very beginning of the second visit, I have been thanked lavishly for my help. Often, this has occurred after initial sessions in which I felt I offered very little—no interpretations, no answers, no suggestions. Inevitably, when I have asked what was most helpful about the visit, the answer would be: "That's the first time in a year that someone has sat with me for an hour and listened to what *I* had to say," or, "I could tell that you were trying to understand me," or, "You didn't give any easy answers. When I cry in front of my girl friend or my parents, they tell me how much I have to be happy about and I can tell they don't understand me." No matter what the client's problem or emotion, no matter how puzzled you might be, your efforts to empathize will be seen and felt by the client and will be a source of inspiration and growth.

COMPOSURE

Many writers (e.g., Bowlby, 1977; Bruch, 1974; Rogers, 1942, 1961) have stated explicitly that therapists must be composed. It is necessary that you be comfortable in your relationship with the client, no matter what he or she says. To the extent that you are uncomfortable with or frightened by a feeling or situation that is described to you, your effectiveness is limited. Conversely, many will find your composure reassuring. Often, people will mention reluctantly a thought, feeling, or incident that they have not shared with anyone previously. If you react calmly, further exploration will follow; if you react with even the slightest detectable discomfort or apprehension, further examination of the issue will be unlikely. Moreover, this reaction may confirm the client's belief that he or she is "crazy," that you cannot help, or that your office is not a safe place to discuss feelings.

Along these lines, Wenegrat (1976), in a study of 34 therapy tape segments, found that accurate empathy ratings were highly correlated with therapist ability to deal comfortably with client emotions. Since, as Spensley and Blacker (1977) have pointed out, most individuals in therapy are struggling with intense emotions that they do not have a satisfactory setting to explore, it is vital that the therapist allow such exploration.

It is also important that you attend to your own emotional state as well as that of your clients. If a certain feeling or issue (e.g., sexual concerns or self-destructive impulses) arouses noticeable discomfort within you, you should consider referring clients who are struggling with it until you overcome the discomfort. Then, with the help of a colleague, supervisor, therapist, counselor, or consultant, make an active effort to overcome this discomfort, so that you might be as helpful as possible to a broad range of people. Clients do not like to be "bounced around" from one counselor to another and may not follow through on a referral, regardless of its appropriateness. In all likelihood, they will feel rejected by you and will be unwilling to take such a risk again.

If you are not able to articulate which feelings or issues cause you to lose your composure, pay particular attention to those times that you offer information and advice. Such a maneuver directs discussion to *your* ideas and opinions—a far step from the client's emotions and struggles. Predictably, in an analogue study using 90 college students, (Ehrlich, D'Angelli, & Danish, 1979) it was found that advice from a therapist discouraged affective responses from clients. Moreover, you should not presume that you are withholding something helpful when you do not offer advice or information. Malett, Spokane, and Vance (1978), for example, found that provision of vocationally relevant information to 40 college students regarding their career plans had no effect on those plans. Clients rarely come to therapists with the primary goal of obtaining facts and information. Further, presenting yourself as a needed source of knowledge usually will be antithetical to an overriding goal of treatment—termination as soon as possible, with the client independent from you.

Typically, the literature regarding composure emphasizes the need for the therapist to be composed in the face of intense anger or sexual feelings. Often overlooked is the need to be comfortable with a considerable amount of uncertainty, confusion, and possibly bizarre ideas or behavior. For, if things are going well, your discussions will lead to those feelings and experiences about which the client is least certain. When this occurs, keep in mind that you are a therapist, a counselor, not a detective or attorney. Any direct interrogation will be counterproductive (Paul, 1976) and, most likely, will be experienced as a challenge. As with advice and information, use an impulse to ask "why" to point the way to a source of discomfort within yourself.

Paradoxically, this need to tolerate uncertainty comfortably is most apparent when the "presenting problem" seems highly dependent on matters of fact. For example, regarding counseling a rape victim, Pepitone-Rockwell (1978) states:

> *Don't try to determine the validity of the rape.* Any determination of rape is made in a legal sense. If you question the victim's story in a legal manner, you are subtly or directly judging her and she is apt to feel more guilty and responsible. . . . If this is a continuing personal style, reconsider your motives [p. 525].

Or, if you are trying to help someone accused of a crime, if *you* ask the person if he or she "did it," from that point on, that client probably will view you as an adversary, someone who is like the others, not trusting. This will happen even if you think you are asking the question for different reasons and if you intend to keep the answer confidential.

As implied above, there will be times when a client's feelings will need to be controlled within the therapeutic relationship. Such limit-setting will be necessary if you and, more importantly, the client are to feel calm and safe. Most likely, this will occur regarding suicidal (Bratter, 1975) or homicidal behavior, other expressions of anger, or intimate or sexual feelings. Your reassurance that emotions can be discussed in depth and detail with the certainty that they will not be overwhelming or acted upon will prove invaluable.

Some individuals, for example, will find great comfort in the knowledge that, no matter what, your relationship will not involve touching. There is a broad continuum here ranging from hand-holding and a "reassuring" pat on the back to sexual intercourse. You should rarely—if ever—initiate touching, and it is likely to be helpful if you discuss with the client any of his or her attempts to do so. To do otherwise is to open the door to misunderstanding. "Touching a person can mean many things, for example, an expression of caring, a desire for intimacy, sexual attraction, or dominance [Alagna, Sheryle, Fisher, & Wicas, 1979, p. 465]."

Schaffer (1980) discusses this point in valuable detail, with appreciation for this issue's complexity:

> Whether or not you ever touch a client, touch is interpreted quite differently by most men and women. If you are a female clinician and touch a male client, he is, because of socialization expectations, likely to interpret the touch as having sexual connotations. If you touch a child or another woman, it may be considered "more appropriate" by the client, but it may also be interpreted as sexual or as "motherly" or patronizing. If you are a male clinician and touch a male client, he may have a very negative reaction because men are not used to being touched, especially by other men. On the other hand, if you touch a

woman client, it may be interpreted as patronizing or as sexual, but the woman will probably not have a negative reaction unless she feels very threatened. Similarly, a male clinician who touches a child will usually be considered patronizing or "fatherly." The important issue is to be aware of your own feelings or justification for touching or not touching a client and to be aware of how touch is interpreted differently by different clients. Try to get in "touch" with your feelings about how you would react to various clients touching you. Do you like clients to touch you, or perhaps some clients and not others, or do you dislike being touched by any client at any time? You need to understand your own feelings and expectations before you can effectively help other people deal with theirs [pp. 46–47].

If, for example, you think it might be helpful to hold a client's hand at a particular moment, say so, in lieu of reaching for the hand without explanation. Among other benefits, this will serve as an example, inviting the client to discuss emotions with you. In fact, acting on rather than discussing and understanding intense emotions may be a significant source of discomfort that has led many people to you. This can include individuals whose relationships with family and friends are stormy and combative, self-destructive and suicidal people, and some individuals whose sexual activity is heightened. Such people often utilize overt expression of affect to maintain emotional distance from others; such physical activity can preclude emotional involvement. Thus, paradoxically, you set the stage for increased communication as you make it clear that all touching is "off limits."

One client, who, at a time of deep sorrow, asked that I hold her, later told me that she was very grateful that I did not. She went on to say that if I had held her, she would have stopped talking in that highly emotional session in which she spoke of previously unacknowledged thoughts and feelings and consequently learned a great deal. You will help clients gain control over troublesome emotions and learn to be comfortable in an intimate relationship with you, if you refrain from touching. Further, the client eventually will be able to bring this composure into other relationships after it is achieved with you.

READINESS TO DISCUSS EVERYTHING

The helper's readiness to discuss everything introduced to the relationship by the client is a unique feature of the therapeutic relationship. Some friends or family can be empathic and composed at times of difficulty, but they are less prepared to discuss the significance and implications of the client's thoughts, feelings, and actions. The therapist does this by design, hoping that the insight gained will help alleviate the suffering that led to the client's seeking professional help. Many distinguished therapists and writers of diverse background and training have made this point (Bruch, 1974; Maier, 1978; Orlinsky & Howard, 1978; Strupp, 1978; Tolbert, 1978).

Examination of a seemingly minute detail may lead to a revelation. And, as Beier (1966) has pointed out and discussed so clearly, many individuals will introduce the most important topics as though they are unimportant. Highly significant material at times will be introduced unwittingly as incidental or "extratherapeutic" in an attempt to keep it unrecognized by and thus safe from the therapist. Appointment changes, issues regarding payment, and requests to change frequency of visits are examples of details that may conceal highly significant issues. There doubtless will be times when discussion of a detail will be inappropriate. "There is no time for reflection when the wastepaper basket is on fire [Beier, 1966, p. 92]." But, such events will be few and far between.

So, think twice before responding to comments such as "I'm tired, why don't you start today?" or, "Do you mind if I pay your bill a week late this month?" or, "Can we skip next week, I'll be out of town?" or, "Can we meet a little longer next time? We always waste so much time getting started." Issues and emotions of critical significance may be concealed by such comments and will remain unrecognized if you respond concretely to the request to get on to more important matters.

Each event and comment that fades into the background without discussion weakens the foundation on which your relationship is based. Open, precise communication about each topic that the client introduces—directly or indirectly—is the heart and soul of successful psychotherapy and counseling. Kemp (1967), for example, states, *"Knowledge is necessary, but for the counselor, it is not enough* [p. 199]." He adds that the counselor must offer an understanding, "that comes from person-to-person encounter in which each relinquishes the facade of his personage. . . . It is not enough to associate, we must communicate [p. 199]."

As Kemp implies, communication skills, honesty, and an unflinching readiness to discuss everything that the client brings up may well override technical skills and theoretical knowledge in importance. When discussing marital-family therapy, Gurman and Kniskern (1978) write, "Therapist relationship skills have major impact on the outcome of . . . treatment regardless of the 'school' orientation of the clinician [p. 884]." Jourard's *The Transparent Self* (1971) is an eloquent plea for workers to be honest and authentic in all of their dealings with clients. To the extent that you avoid discussion of any topic, you limit your effectiveness. "While simple honesty with others (and thus to oneself) may produce scars, it is likely to be an effective preventive of both mental illness and certain kinds of physical sickness. Honesty can literally be a health insurance policy [p. 133]." By attending to those issues and emotions most difficult for the client to discuss, you simultaneously help him or her confront those matters that are most bothersome and that led that person to your office. Strupp (1977) underscores the absolute necessity of discussing troublesome, *"meaningful patterns that come alive in the patient-therapist relationship* in vivo [p. 17]."

As Freud has pointed out, and as others have echoed over the years, at times you will need to respond to what is being "said" nonverbally. Some clients tentatively will, in this manner, introduce sensitive material. Freud (1905/1953) wrote:

> He that has eyes to see and ears to hear may convince himself that no mortal can keep a secret. If the lips are silent, he chatters with his finger tips; betrayal oozes out of him at every pore. And thus the task of making conscious the most hidden recesses of the mind is one which it is quite possible to accomplish [pp. 77–78].

You do not have to accept Freud's theory of unconscious motivation to acknowledge the importance of nonverbal communication. Laboratory research, not relying on psychoanalytic principles or techniques, supports this point of view. For example, Norton (1978), using Carkhuff's Scales of Interpersonal Functioning, found that counselors who used information gained from nonverbal behaviors were more effective and sensitive to client concerns than counselors who did not.

Finally, seemingly subtle changes in speech also may direct you and the client to fruitful areas of discussion. For example, Nelson and Groman (1978) found that many individuals "flee the present" in stressful situations by using fewer present tense verbs. Similarly, certain individuals will shift from words such as "I" or "me" to words such as "it" or "this" when the topic at hand is particularly difficult to discuss. For example, a person having difficulty acknowledging discouragement may say, "Doctor, do you think this is getting anything accomplished?" Or, someone else may find it easier to say, "It's so silly," or "It's so confusing," rather than "I feel silly," or, "I am confused."

Your intentional, deliberate willingness to discuss everything fully—even the most sensitive or seemingly unimportant topics—often will lead the way to important feelings that have been disguised or overlooked. Effective therapy, as Fenichel (1945) has pointed out, teaches the client that "he has nothing to fear in tolerating impulses formerly warded off [p. 570]."

ENCOURAGEMENT

Another characteristic of effective helpers is that they fully believe that each client is capable of functioning at a higher level—emotionally and interpersonally—than manifest at the initial meeting (Adams, 1977; Olin, 1976;

Padow, 1977–1978). It is difficult to imagine your being helpful without such optimism. Indeed, your unwavering confidence in the client's potential may be the most important characteristic that you bring to the relationship. "A therapist is a person who plans to make a patient feel that there is more to him than he thinks [Friedman, 1976, p. 268]." Jourard (1968) writes, "Successful therapeutic outcome is not a function of the techniques employed as such; rather, it is an outcome of such matters as the therapist's faith in the potential for fuller functioning [p. 62]."

One way or another, try to communicate this confidence. For many, the absence of such much-needed encouragement will have been a large factor in their downslide before meeting you. Your encouragement will "inspire the patient with confidence that he or she is in the right place [and give the] expectation that good things will happen [Cousins, 1979, p. 154]." This encouragement will counteract the helpless feeling that is the main problem of most clients (Bruch, 1974).

Hope can be communicated in a variety of ways and should be offered at the first meeting. With some, a direct comment such as "You don't deserve to be treated the way he's treating you," or, "I'm glad that you've come to speak with me. I think things can be much better for you," is all that will be needed. In fact, some people have told me that they began to feel better after making their first appointment but before meeting me. Knowing that the first appointment is just a few days away can be a source of strength and optimism.

Many people will receive invaluable encouragement from what you do *not* say. For example, some will be reassured when you do not introduce topics such as hospitalization and medication. Others will be strengthened by your confidently ending a meeting on time. They may believe something like, "If she's willing to have me leave now and not see me again for a week knowing what I've just told her, things must not be so bad. Maybe I'm not so crazy after all!" Finally, explicit therapeutic goals and progress toward them—regardless of their nature—often are a source of inspiration.

PURPOSEFULNESS

Increasingly, it is becoming clear that it is desirable to work with the client toward identified goals (Goldberg, 1975). After the areas most in need of change have been identified, do all you can to help the client make those changes, while viewing yourself as a provider of short-term assistance. Maier (1978) writes, "The helper does not change people (nor could anyone else do such a trick). Rather, the helper creates conditions predictively that enable the individual client(s) involved to develop their capacity for changing selected aspects of their particular life situations [p. 222]."

No matter how specific (e.g., "I'm petrified of automobiles") or how general (e.g., "I feel awful") the problem, you will be most helpful to the great majority of clients if you provide short-term, purposeful counseling. Help the client do the work to be done. Then, "get out of the way" so that he or she can resume life without you. Otherwise, you will become involved in relationships that are comfortable but are also protracted, aimless, and, in the end, harmful. Such relationships encourage the client to think that he or she needs you when that is not the case.

In other words, one explicit counseling goal—with everyone—should be termination (Goldberg, 1975; Spensley & Blacker, 1977). It is a mistake to assume that we are doing well when a client remains in treatment, month after month, sometimes year after year. Similarly, it is wrong to believe that if treatment has been very brief (e.g., six or eight visits—or even one or two), it has failed. Terms such as "flight into health" and "transference cure" reflect the widespread bias that, by and large, the more meetings we have with each client, the more we are helping (Rosenthal, 1966). In fact, the opposite may be true. Evidence from a variety of sources, using a variety of measures is abundant that short-term therapy is *as*, if not *more*, effective than long-term (Albin, 1980; de la Torre, 1978; Donovan & Mitchell, 1979; Gevinson, 1977; Gurman & Kniskern, 1978; June, 1979; Keilson, Dworkin, & Gelso, 1979; Mann, 1973; Marmor, 1979; Strassberg, Anchor, Cunningham, & Elkins, 1977).

Further, regardless of your intentions, you probably will average less than eight visits with most of the people that you see (Butcher & Koss, 1978; Koss, 1979; Strupp, 1978a, p. 17). This fact underscores the wisdom of clients, who seem to see us as sources of short-term help, even though many therapists associate termination after a short time with failure. "Intentional" is the term used by Ivey and Simek-Downing (1980, p. 8) to describe the purposeful, goal-directed helper who resists counterproductive, long-term relationships with clients.

SUMMARY AND CONCLUSIONS

In summary, the helpful counselor or therapist is one who is empathic, composed in the face of intense emotions, ready to discuss everything, encouraging, and purposeful. Further, he or she is oriented toward helping the client define and achieve these goals and then to discontinue the visits. Ruesch (1973) stated this another way when he wrote that therapists and counselors need "to understand, to acknowledge, and to reply [p. 31]." Many experienced, well-intentioned, ethical workers do not possess these abilities. Such abilities are not easy to come by, and, once achieved, conscious effort is needed to maintain them. Otherwise, we may slip back to less helpful ways of relating. Perhaps this is what Gendlin had in mind when he said, "Just because two people are talking in a room and one is called a doctor and the other is labelled a patient, it does not mean that psychotherapy is occurring [cited in Karon and VandenBos, 1975, p. 148]."

Although these five characteristics are highly desirable, they will not assure your effectiveness as a counselor. You must offer the client more. Certain friends and family members can possess the five characteristics described above, and a person may be miserable nonetheless. A theoretical orientation is necessary and provides a foundation for your work, but your effectiveness will not be determined by *which* orientation you prefer. Many now acknowledge that the relative merits of various theories has been overrated in importance and that your flexibility is as desirable as adherence to a particular orientation (Corey, Corey & Callanan, 1979; Cummings, 1979; McGhee, 1979; Schimel, 1980). Although all theoretical orientations are "the best" according to their proponents, none of them has demonstrated superiority over any other over time, even when studies are restricted to a particular "presenting problem" for which one approach seems most suited.

Also, a variety of well-respected clinicians now discourage excessive emphasis upon techniques. For example, Rogers (1961) has stated that the attitudes and feelings of the therapist are more important than techniques and methods. (This comment is particularly significant, since so many workers are certain of the value—or lack thereof—of a "Rogerian" approach.) Strupp (1978a), after examining a very broad range of studies, concluded, "So far, it has not been possible to show that one technique is clearly superior to another, even under reasonably controlled conditions [p. 11]." Jourard, (1968) another well-known therapist and scholar, wrote, "Effective psychotherapists, who succeed in inviting sufferers to change their previous ways of being, are not technicians [pp. 57–58]." And, Corey et al. (1979) have concluded that "the personal attributes of the therapist [are] the single most important determinant of successful therapy [p. 24]."

Moreover, the various therapeutic approaches are by no means as distinct as some would have us believe. For example, Murray and Jacobson (1978) have pointed out that techniques within a school often vary more than techniques between certain schools. Deikman and Whitaker (1979) report a study in which a "drug-oriented" hospital ward was converted to a psychotherapy-oriented one. One finding of this study was that:

> While our theoretical orientation was, in our minds, that of psychoanalytic ego psychology, a psychologist trained in gestalt therapy felt strongly that we were doing gestalt therapy; another psychologist, an acknowledged "expert" in behavior therapy, insisted that we were doing behavior therapy [p. 212].

In a study by Fiedler (1950), nondirective, psychoanalytic, and eclectic therapists were asked to describe the ideal therapeutic relationship. Statistically significant, positive correlations were found among the descriptions of the three therapist groups. All stated the necessity of an empathic relationship, good patient-therapist relations, mutual trust, and an ability of the therapist to stay close to the client's problems. Many others (Hoen-Saric, 1977; Mahoney & Arnkoff, 1978; Sloane, Staples, Cristol, Yorkston & Whipple, 1975; Strupp, 1979; Wachtel, 1977) have underscored crucial similarities among a number of "distinct" schools of therapy.

Indeed, excessive adherence to the techniques associated with a school—particularly a "new" or "faddish" one—may reflect insecurity, even ineptness, on the part of the counselor. For example, in the Fiedler study described above, it was found that expert counselors representing different approaches were more similar to one another than experienced and inexperienced counselors within a particular school. Patterson (1980) would have us declare a moratorium on additional approaches to therapy. He writes:

> When, however, one looks at the characteristics of the new approaches, they appear to have one thing in common: they involve the counsellor or therapist as expert, actively engaged in techniques of a directive, controlling type, resulting in a vertical relationship with the client. This constitutes a reversion to earlier more authoritarian approaches. To the extent that they are successful it is mainly through the immediate but usually temporary placebo effect, which is maximized by suggestion and the counsellor's authority and prestige [p. 107].

Patterson adds that such approaches appeal most to "counsellors who lack respect for or confidence in the client [p. 107]."

During an informal question and answer session, Jourard (1968) stated, "I think it's possible for people even nitwits to go through a training program like a master of his techniques, but remain nitwits. They may be technically competent counselors and therapists who are yet uneducated boobs [p. 78]." He added that to be a psychotherapist one must be "as flexible, inventive, and creative as law, ethics and the dignity and integrity and well-being of oneself and one's patient will allow. And that leaves much elbow-room [p. 97]."

I agree with those who have noted that we have overlooked the importance of certain events and decisions that inevitably arise in psychotherapy (e.g., Gottsegen & Gottsegen, 1979). Evidence indicates that the manner in which you treat these issues defines your relationship with clients and, in large part, determines your effectiveness. These ingredients are discussed in the following chapters, and your helpfulness will be increased greatly if your work reflects an understanding of the unique impact they have on your efforts.

In other words, possession of the five qualities described in this chapter is not enough. Helpers who more or less equally possess these qualities vary greatly in their effectiveness. The empathic, composed, encouraging, purposeful therapist who is attentive and ready to discuss everything is like the capable teacher who "knows the material" and comes to class prepared to present a good lecture but whose work fails to reflect an appreciation for the subtleties, complexities, and tensions inherent in the student-teacher relationship. Such teachers may have mastered the mechanics of teaching, but they often lack flexibility and are blind to what they can learn from "students." Such teachers are forgotten quickly.

Chapter 2
The First Meeting

A bad beginning makes a bad ending.
— Euripides, *Aeolus*, Fragment 32

Legally, the therapist has a duty to communicate to
the client an honest representation of his skills and
methods, along with the conditions of therapy. Fees,
appointment schedules, and special obligations of both
therapist and client are also part of the understanding.
— Van Hoose and Kottler, 1977

Your first meeting with each client is of special significance. If for no other reason, this is true because the first meeting may also be the last, and thus your only opportunity to help the client. Regardless of your skill, your wishes, your recommendations, or the intensity of a client's distress, some people will not return for a second visit. Although you should avoid overestimating your importance to clients, it is important to keep in mind that comments you make during your first visit—especially if it is your only one —may have a lasting influence.

Moreover, a client's first impressions of you will influence whether or not a second appointment is made. And, if the client does not return, he or she probably will be less willing to see other therapists in the future. Conversely, if you are perceived as helpful at the first meeting, a second visit is likely to follow, and the client is likely to make positive comments about such a helping relationship to friends and family who, at some future point, may consider entering counseling.

In fact, significant decisions about you may be made by a client before the first visit. One individual, when explaining why she was able to enter a type of relationship with me that she had been unable to achieve previously, said, "I knew you were the kind of person who could help me. When I first phoned to speak to you, you weren't in, and your secretary told me to phone you at home. When I phoned, I could tell that you weren't bothered by my call and that you weren't rushing me. Even though we hadn't met, I could tell that you cared."

Many people will not have the persistence to return for a second visit if they do not perceive you as uniquely helpful at the first. Since you are virtual strangers at this point, they may be reluctant to discuss such a disappointment frankly. They are more likely to assume that *they* did something wrong, that psychotherapy is not for them, or that their problem is either too trivial or too complicated for such discussions. Any one of these conclusions may result in the decision to terminate. Although a client may appear satisfied with the first meeting, he or she may leave thinking, "I'll never go see him again! He stared at me for an hour, didn't say much, and, when it was over, charged me $50 and asked if I wanted to come back next week." On the other hand, after a successful first visit, therapy can be well under way. The client may leave thinking, "It was great! I felt she really understood me, was comfortable with me and my problem, and we've started to look for solutions together."

Importantly, the unhelpful therapist may think he has done very well. He may have been pleased with the degree of affect the client expressed and with the insights he was beginning to develop about the client. But, at a first meeting, you must offer much more than your undisclosed insights and formulations, your time, your attention, and a setting for the client to express feelings. It is important that you clarify to the client at least some of the distinguishing features of your relationship. Otherwise, the client may leave without adequate reason to return.

Since many clients will come to you at considerable personal and financial expense, they will not be likely to come regularly for weeks or months waiting to discover what you have to offer that caring friends and relatives do not. For many, the decision to see you will not have been made lightly and will be a very big step, with considerable hope and expectation associated with it. As a result of seeing you, some people may be ridiculed or thought of as "mentally ill." Further, they may be perceived as "weak" or may lose or fail to get a job or be overlooked for promotion because they are "mentally ill." It can be a severe disappointment to take these and similar risks to see you and then spend 50 minutes or so "just talking" about a problem, an emotion, a circumstance that, in many cases, they already will have discussed at length with others and can continue to discuss with them.

Consequently, at the first visit, it is vital that you discuss the distinguishing features of your relationship. These features are: your profession, client expectations, time and cost, housekeeping, and the contract. Regardless of a client's "presenting problem," the setting in which you work, or your approach to counseling, the way in which you treat these five issues defines your therapeutic relationships. Early discussion of these issues *is* the start of therapy. The client will come to you with questions and feelings about these issues, and it is incumbent upon you to see to it that these issues are discussed.

Through such discussion you will both clarify the unique role you may play in the person's life and set the stage for confronting whatever is most important at each meeting. If you accomplish this together, successful psychotherapy will be under way; if you set these topics aside to discuss "more important" issues, the opposite will be true.

Often it will not be possible to discuss fully each of these five issues at the first meeting. Some clients may sob for thirty minutes and experience it as extremely insensitive if you insist on discussing, say, a therapeutic contract. Others may talk hurriedly for the first half hour, presenting information that they desperately want you to know and that they have been rehearsing from the moment they made the appointment. When these issues do not get discussed at the first meeting, mention them, indicating that you wish to discuss them at the next meeting. For example, you might say, "We didn't discuss my fee today. Let's be sure to do that next time." Or, as suggested by Bruch (1974), you might schedule your first visits to be twice as long as the others.

YOUR PROFESSION

Perhaps the most distinguishing feature of the therapeutic relationship is that it is a professional one. Your roles as helper and professional are inseparable. "Becoming a psychotherapist is intricately interwoven with developing a professional identity, and represents, at the same time, a broadening of one's individuality and maturation as a person [Bruch, 1974, p. 84]." Usually, you will be the only person talking with the client about personal problems in a professional capacity. Since your relationship with a client is fundamentally professional rather than personal, you can help in a way that others cannot (Strupp, 1978). Clarification of this point is, in fact, a necessary component of this help.

Unfortunately, many consumers associate professionalism with indifference and self-interest. Permit the client to know that you do not intend to be impersonal and dispassionate, that the word "professional" does not mean being "without feeling in the fact of human misery [Jourard, 1971, p. 197]." Permit the client to know that your professional organization exists primarily for the protection and benefit of him or her—not yourself. Sadly, as London (1964) points out, this fact has been overshadowed because, historically, most professional groups have attended to their own concerns at the expense of their clients'.

Counseling will be facilitated if you inform the client of the more honorable characteristics of your profession. For example, most professions have ethical codes, designed to protect the client (Flexner, 1915; Jacobs, 1976; Kinney & Leaton, 1978). The best way to let people know of these protections is to have available in quantity in your office or reception area copies of your ethical code. Be sure each client receives a copy by the first visit and is encouraged to read it and ask questions about it. Undoubtedly, the code will answer questions that the client may be reluctant to ask or may not have time to ask (e.g., questions regarding confidentiality, sexual involvement, your area of expertise). Do not overlook the relevance of the fact that you are part of a profession that has been developing for generations and has been struggling to answer these questions in ways most beneficial to the client.

Along similar lines, Morrison (1979, 1980) suggests that all therapists or agencies have a client advisory board or consumer protection board to respond to certain client questions and grievances. Many people will be more willing to approach this group than a professional ethics committee or board. And, with certain questions or issues, a board of current and former clients potentially will be more helpful and appropriate than a professional committee.

A second characteristic of professional workers is that they not only assume responsibility for the quality of their work (Flexner, 1915; Michels, 1980; Peterson, 1976; Wilcox, 1964), but also for the setting of standards in the workplace (Kinney & Leaton, 1978). Clients may pay a great deal of attention to oversights or procedures that seem unimportant to you. For example, modes of address are very important. You, the client, and other workers (e.g., secretaries and maintenance workers) should be addressed with equal respect and courtesy. If you wish to be addressed as "Dr. Smith" or "Ms. Johnson," address clients and secretaries as "Ms.," "Mr.," or whatever mode of address is appropriate to them. It may present insurmountable problems if you say, "I'm Dr. Johnson, come in, Mary" at the start of your first visit with a twenty-year-old woman. At a first visit, many clients will note such events and react to them privately. Unless your visit is with a very young child, introduce yourself and ask how he or she wishes to be addressed (Bruch, 1974). Nontherapeutic attitudes can be revealed by overly friendly or patronizing modes of address.

Also, as Shertzer and Stone (1980) point out, "The setting in which counseling is conducted undoubtedly has some bearing on whether the relationship will be facilitated or thwarted [p. 25]." At a first meeting especially, clients will attend to such things as room size, seating arrangements, perceived privacy, and availability of restrooms. Although very few studies have been done in this area—referred to as "proxemics"—those that have been done support this point of view. For example, Holahan and Slaikeu (1977) found that client self-disclosure at a first meeting decreased as privacy decreased. The three levels of privacy used were a separate room, a room separated from an adjoining room by a partition, and a room in which a third person entered for a moment during the session.

Even your attire is likely to influence a clients' anxiety level at the first meeting. Hubble and Gelso (1978) found that "clients experienced significantly lower anxiety with counselor in casual versus highly casual attire [p. 581]." No difference was found between traditional and casual attire. (In this study, which needs to be repeated using women counselors, "traditional" attire was coat and tie, "casual" was sport shirt and slacks, and "highly casual" was sweat shirt and jeans.) The authors also found that *"clients manifest the most desirable reactions to counselors who dress in a way that is one step or level more formal than the client's own dress level* [p. 584]."

Along similar lines, clients should know that confidentiality means more to you than a reluctance to discuss "cases" with your family. For example, do not use public sign-in sheets in your office. Whenever possible, avoid using surnames of clients within earshot of other clients, and have secretaries do the same. Make sure that typed or written notes are not left on a desk or in a typewriter within eyesight of any client. I remember vividly a particular first meeting that went very well. I later learned that, when this person was leaving the office, she noticed (although she had to tilt her head upside-down to do so) a note being typed that had another individual's name on it. Almost a year later, at another setting, the client told me that she never returned for a second visit because she assumed that if I was that "careless" about the identity of one person, I might not treat information about her carefully enough either.

You cannot be too attentive to these types of details. They contribute to your definition as a professional worker. This is particularly true at the first meeting, when one of the main decisions a client will make is whether or not to return, and when the client has minimal opportunity to get to know you as a person. You are much more likely to be perceived as a potential source of help if you consider these details carefully. Carelessness surrounding such details has been one of the contributing factors in the current wave of antiprofessionalism (Michels, 1980) and will limit unnecessarily your ability to help.

CLIENT EXPECTATIONS

Every client will enter the first meeting with unique expectations. If you do not develop some understanding of these expectations during the first visit, the client will be disappointed. Conversely, if you develop such an understanding, you simultaneously will be demonstrating a sensitivity to that person's uniqueness. Unless you feel the person is beyond your help, or that such help is inappropriate, it is extremely important that you respond to these expectations at the first meeting.

This process will require all of the necessary therapist characteristics described in chapter 1. If the client is to discuss expectations freely, you will need to be composed, empathic, and prepared to discuss anything; your encouragement and purposefulness will be demonstrated as you offer help. Thus, understanding and responding to client expectations at the first visit is part of the start of therapy. If you overlook this step or are casual about a client's expectations, successful treatment is unlikely to follow.

Some general observations can be made about client expectations. For example, most of the people who come to you will be hoping that you help them in some way. Thus, any offer of help is likely to increase the client's morale (Murray & Jacobson, 1978). Some individuals will come to you under duress. Your attempts to discern such a client's limited expectations will make this clear to you and may allow you to be of some assistance to this individual. At the very least, this will help avoid many frustrating sessions in which you both are working at cross-purposes. Do not feel that you need to offer some profound insight, suggestion, or observation at the first visit. At times, "all" the help you will need to offer is the reassurance that the client has come to the right place (Cousins, 1979). At other times, an optimistic comment or a calm response will prove invaluable.

The first words you hear from a client may be something like, "I'm not sure I've come to the right place, but . . ." or, "I'm not sure you can help me, but let me tell you what's bothering me." Do not overlook such comments to get to "important" material. Regardless of what follows, if you do not offer some reassurance at that point, the client may leave the first visit believing that you, too, have overriding doubts about the potential helpfulness of the relationship.

At times, a client's expectations will differ greatly from what you might expect. This difference, if not detected promptly, will be the beginning of misunderstandings which will result in confusion, frustration, and early termination. For example, regarding drug abusers, Cummings (1979) writes, "Addicts do not come to us to be helped for their addiction. They come to us because they are about to lose something or have lost something. . . . They come wanting the therapist to bring back the halcyon days when drugs worked and made them feel mellow [pp. 1122–1123]." Kupst and Schulman (1979) report broad discrepancies between professional and lay expectations of the helping relationship. Their study revealed differences between the two groups regarding "degree of expected change, importance of self in problem-solving, financial emphasis, and expected duration of psychotherapy [p. 237]." Kupst and Schulman concluded that premature termination occurs most commonly as a result of differences between what most clients expect from therapy and what they receive. Other authors, working with a variety of clients in diverse settings, have arrived at this same conclusion (Frank, 1973; Kamin & Coughlin, 1963).

Gelso (1979) has noted that "nearly all people who enter therapy do so, to varying degrees, with the wish (conscious or unconscious demand) to have dependent longings and affectional needs gratified *in the therapy itself* [p. 276]." He provides useful suggestions regarding gratification of such demands. Although you may not agree with Gelso's opinion, it does underscore the need to discuss what each person wants from you.

Most clients will expect you to get to know them in a way others do not. Especially during the first few visits, when you and the client do not know each other very well, take pains to explain yourself very clearly, and allow the client to do the same. For example, "I'm depressed" means different things to different people. The word "depression" can be an attempt to communicate sadness, confusion, desperation, despondency, guilt, anger, etc. In an early session, when a client says, "I'm depressed," say, "How do you feel when you're depressed?" or, "What does that word mean to you?" Such a response will demonstrate your wish to understand the person beyond a typical conversational level.

TIME AND COST

Only rarely will a client come to you without important expectations and questions regarding two particular issues—time and money. Typical questions are: How much do these visits cost? Will my insurance pay for it? When will this meeting end? How often may I come?

If you discuss such matters promptly, you set the stage for examination of each and every issue that comes up, no matter how awkward. First, it is a good idea to let the client know as soon as possible the length of a typical visit and that you will not be interrupted unless there is an emergency. A client may be unable to take full advantage of, say, a fifty minute, uninterrupted visit, if he or she does not know the length of the visit. Some will avoid discussion of a certain issue, perhaps the very one that led them to you, lest they be interrupted precipitously. Discussion of "time" will result in more effective use of it.

A particular first session with a young woman who came to see me almost immediately after a traumatic sexual experience comes to mind. The meeting was a very cathartic one for her, and I felt I was at my best during it. I was very puzzled when she did not appear for her second session; in fact, she never returned to see me again. Many months later, a close friend of hers told me that the woman did not return because she was very angry that she was not allowed to talk with me for as long as she wished. Even though the session lasted fifty minutes and it seemed appropriate to stop, the client felt rejected, perceived me as insensitive, and was startled at my wish to bring the meeting to a close.

Regardless of the length of a visit, be involved fully with the client for its entirety. Do not allow telephone or other interruptions unless there is a *bona fide* emergency. Do not schedule too many appointments in one day. If you do, you may find yourself thinking of your previous or next appointment when you are "with" someone. Your effectiveness will be limited if you do not use your time suitably. Indeed, each client deserves more time from you than the time actually spent with you. A clear mind before each visit and a carefully written or dictated note after each visit is a necessity. Corey, Corey, and Callanan (1979) speak of a colleague who allows one hour before each group meeting "to get himself in focus before his group arrives [p. 178]."

There will be rare occasions when you will have to end a meeting prematurely because of an emergency regarding another client. The few clients who have been interrupted by me in this manner have been understanding and have been reassured by the interruption. Typically, one client said, "I'm glad you asked to end our meeting early to help someone else. It made me feel helpful, too, and I know now that if *I* ever need you in a real hury, you'll be there."

Creative and flexible use of time is a necessity; your helpfulness will not be in direct proportion to the time spent with a client. For example, a member of a group of drug abusers once said to Cummings (1979), "Nick, you are never going to help us as long as we are hitting. . . . Whether we see you once a week, twice a week, three times a week, or every day, hitting is so pleasurable, we can wipe out all the therapy you give us with one pill or a touch of the needle [p. 1123]." The traditional "therapeutic hour" will not be right for everyone. Some will benefit most from shorter meetings, some from longer. Some will respond best to biweekly or monthly meetings; some may require brief, daily visits for a while.

Along these lines, it has been found that many clients react negatively if they are told that the maximum number of sessions they might have with you is limited, even if the stated limit is significantly greater than the average number of sessions after which most people terminate voluntarily (Koss, 1979; McKitrick & Gelso, 1978).

Cousins (1979) was speaking of physicians when he wrote the following, but his words are true for therapists and counselors as well. "Time is the one thing patients need most from their doctors—time to be heard, time to have things explained, time to be reassured. . . . Yet the one thing that too many doctors find most difficult to command or manage is time [p. 137]."

Clients pay a high price for the time spent with you, and this cost should be discussed. This cost is relevant regardless of your fee or the client's financial circumstances. One dollar paid for a clinic visit may be more, proportionately, than fifty dollars paid by someone else for a private visit. Further, there are "costs" in addition to direct financial cost. Some people may have to drive through rush-hour traffic for an hour to see you. Others may have to make complicated arrangements with family, employers, or day-care workers. Still others will pay a different kind of price when they tell friends, coworkers, or family that they have decided to see a counselor. It would be a rare client indeed who would not have strong feelings about such costs being paid. Moreover, the financial cost of the visit has implications for what you—and the client—are "worth." Thus, you will find that many individuals will be very reluctant to discuss financial details. In such instances, it becomes particularly important to discuss the client's feelings about the fee being paid.

Since the fee is related directly to the value of the work being done, delinquent bill payment is often a reflection of dissatisfaction with treatment. At some level, many clients seem aware of what Fromm-Reichman pointed out more than three decades ago (1950); your attempts to help are "priceless if successful or worthless if they fail [p. 67]."

Bruch (1974), noting the direct connection between payment problems and therapy problems, writes, "To an amazing degree, difficulties in money matters parallel difficulties in interpersonal relations during the therapy. . . . Nonattention to payment may conceal serious deficits in the progress of therapy [pp. 14–15]." I have found it helpful to have clients pay me directly (either weekly or monthly) rather than pay a secretary or mail payment to me. This has led to my immediate, first-hand realization of the types of difficulties Bruch refers to when they have arisen. Further, this practice demonstrates to the client my readiness to confront all matters relevant to us, no matter how personal or awkward. Many professional workers, in a variety of fields, seem uneasy about the fee they charge and go to great pains to avoid receiving direct payment from consumers.

The few studies done on fees support their relevance to the helping process. Pasternack (1977), for example, found that psychiatry residents failed to consider the relationship between flagrant fee violations and other treatment issues. Pasternack found that presentation of an explicit fee policy led to an increased level of residents' awareness of clients and that therapists' ability to establish fee boundaries was related directly to their ability to establish other boundaries in therapy. Buckley, Karasu, and Charles (1979) concluded from a survey of 20 therapy supervisors that avoidance of fee setting is one of the most common mistakes of beginning therapists.

When you discuss fees, you should discuss policies regarding missed appointments and cancellations. If you intend to charge for such "visits," tell the client well in advance. However, there seems to be no justification for charging a fee for a professional service not rendered. If a client cancels or misses a visit, "see a colleague, write a paper or read a book, which will improve your professional work and professional standing, and thus is in a sense income producing [Steinzor, 1967, p. 195]."

If you work in a setting in which no direct fee is charged, be sensitive to the unique conflicts and resistances that may arise as a result. Nash and Cavenar (1976), for example, found that clients not charged a direct fee may depreciate the value of therapy, feel inappropriately indebted to the therapist, or expect the therapist to make inappropriate nonfinancial demands.

You should not conclude from such a finding that a substantial, direct fee need be charged for all the work you do. If you work in a clinic or other setting in which a direct fee is not charged, or in which the fee is minimal, the client may be paying indirectly for the visits via taxes or through tuition charges if you work at a college or university counseling center. Further, as pointed out above, regardless of monetary costs, most clients will be seeing you at considerable personal cost. What you should conclude from this discussion is that your directness and sensitivity in discussing costs in the early sessions is necessary for effective treatment and is related to your ability to discuss other personal matters on the client's mind, whatever they might be.

HOUSEKEEPING

Time and money matters are but two of many important details associated with your work that may be second nature to you but are totally unknown to a client at the first meeting. Following are some examples—by no means an exhaustive list—of additional questions that might be on the client's mind before or during the first meeting. How often will we meet? Do you take notes? Where are the notes kept? Who can see them? Can I see them? Will my insurance policy at work pay for this? If so, will they pay without telling my boss? What are we supposed to do together? Will you stand by me if I "get worse" or say something you don't like? Do I have to be crazy to come here? How can talking with you help me feel less anxious? Are the meetings *really* confidential?

You may know the answers to all of these questions. The client may know the answer to none of them. And, it would be the rare person, indeed, who would "jump into" therapy without knowing the answers to some of these questions—the ones most important to him or her at the time of the first meeting. To do so would be analogous to diving into an unfamiliar lake without knowing if there are rocks below the surface, the approximate temperature and depth of the water, and if there is a lifeguard on duty. Your effectiveness will be limited greatly if you do not set aside some time at the first visit to discuss whatever "housekeeping" details are most relevant to each client. If you neglect these questions to get to "more important" matters, many clients may terminate prematurely or may be very guarded in their meetings with you, fearing the answers.

Goldberg (1977) found that much of what is viewed as resistance in group therapy, especially in the first meetings, was attributable directly to ignorance of the ground-rules and nature of psychotherapy. Similarly, Garrison (1978) found that group therapy clients who were provided either verbal or written information regarding procedures prior to the first group meeting had better attendance over the first six sessions than those clients who were not provided such information. Also, in an analogue study (Wollersheim, Mcfall, Hamilton, Hickey, & Bordewick, 1980), exposure to a treatment rationale prior to treatment—regardless of whether the approach was Rational Emotive Therapy (RET), psychoanalysis, or behavioristic—"enhanced rated willingness to enter counseling, and promoted a more accurate perception of the nature of psychological problems and the requirements of treatment [p. 225]." The authors concluded that providing precounseling information promoted accurate and positive expectations of counseling.

It is worth repeating that both the Garrison and the Wollersheim et al. studies found written information to be as effective as verbal. For, by now you may be wondering, "How can I possibly discuss all of the issues mentioned in this chapter in the first visit—even if it's two hours long, and even if we don't discuss anything else?" You may wish to have a printed sheet or brochure available in quantity in your reception area, and, where appropriate, mailed to clients immediately after the first appointment is made. Such a document can provide relevant, personal information that also will serve the purpose of encouraging the client to view you as an ally, even before the first meeting. Such a written presentation of a broad range of information is far preferable to presenting it piecemeal. To do the latter is to describe the rules of the game as the game goes along—not at the beginning.

THE CONTRACT

It is a small step from saying that you have an obligation to answer a variety of questions, either verbally or in writing, to saying that there should be a contract between therapist and client. I am in agreement with an increasing number of writers (Adams & Orgel, 1975; Furgeri, 1980; Hare–Mustin, Maracek, Kaplan & Liss-Levinson, 1979) who advocate an explicit contract between therapist and client. This contract need not be a witnessed, notarized document, filed away with other important legal papers. In fact, contracts need not be written to be valid and enforceable.

In all likelihood, you already are entering contractual agreements with clients, even though you may not realize it. A cursory mention of the five components of a contract—offer, acceptance, consideration, competence, and legality—makes this clear. When an individual asks you for help, that is the "offer." Your agreement to help with a particular problem constitutes "acceptance." The "consideration" is what you give each other; most clients, directly or indirectly, give you money, and you, in return, "give" psychotherapy or counseling. "Competence" refers to the fact that an individual must be legally competent to enter into an enforceable contractual agreement. Finally, a contract that is not legal is not enforceable.

Thus, only rarely will therapy begin *without* some sort of contract. What I am advocating is a specific, precise contract, emphasizing whatever issues are most important to a particular client. With some, the limits of confidentiality will need to be articulated. With others, the length of visits, location of visits, or use of the telephone will need to be clarified. Fees, therapeutic goals, and the nature of record keeping should also be agreed upon. Discuss all such issues fully and clearly and honor all agreements reached. "Nothing is more apt to cancel out the experience of a trustworthy and supportive relationship than a therapist who is haphazard in filling his side of the arrangement [Bruch, 1974, p. 12]." An imprecise therapeutic contract that is not taken seriously—regardless of whether it is written—is the start of imprecise therapy that is not taken seriously. Preparation of a contract inevitably will define the tasks of the psychotherapy, of the client, and of the therapist (Borriello, 1979). Attempts to help will be misguided if this early step is omitted.

Chapter 3
The Client's Strengths

> Some to the fascination of a name
> Surrender judgment, hoodwink'd
> > —William Cowper, *The Task*
> > Book vi, Winter Walk at Noon,
> > line 101.

> Most cases are mixed cases, and we should not
> treat our classifications with too much respect.
> > —William James, *Varieties of*
> > *Religious Experience*, 1902,
> > p. 148

ASSESSMENT AND PSYCHOTHERAPY

Your assessment of the client is another process that begins with the first meeting. Most counselors and therapists agree that, without assessment, attempts to help are aimless. Thus, in most settings, counselors assess, classify, or diagnose each client before treatment begins, believing that "planning a treatment program must begin with an accurate diagnostic assessment [American Psychiatric Association, 1980, p. 1]." This quotation is from the most comprehensive, widely-used diagnostic and classification system, the *Diagnostic and statistical manual of mental disorders*, third edition, usually referred to as the "DSM-III." Although the DSM-III is mentioned often below, the comments made regarding the relationship between assessment and therapy apply no matter which classification system is used.

The belief that assessment and counseling are distinct is so pervasive that, in many settings, the "intake" is done by someone other than the eventual therapist. Few have questioned the assumption that assessment and therapy are so easily separable. It was not uncommon for Freud, for example, to meet with an individual for months before deciding whether or not to begin psychoanalysis. More recently, when describing the DSM-III field trials, the following statement appears: "The reliability interviews, with only few exceptions, were initial diagnostic evaluations before treatment was initiated [American Psychiatric Asociation, 1980, p. 467]." Similarly, Thorne (1973) has written that, "If clinical judgment is to evolve beyond intuitive-artistic applications, it must be based solidly on valid diagnoses from which logical indications for case handling can be derived [p. 469]." Most believe that through assessment we answer such questions as: What is this person's problem? How severe is it? Is this child hyperactive? Is counseling likely to be long– or short-term? Is individual or family therapy most appropriate? Is this person well-suited for a group?

Assessment (which typically focuses on discomfort, problems, inadequacies, and doubts) often works in opposition to therapeutic goals. On the one hand, you must find out "where it hurts." On the other hand, your early, excessive attention to problems may preclude your providing the necessary encouragement described in chapter 1. Such a discussion can lead to accurate assessment. It can also serve to make the client more miserable. Appreciation of this possibility has led at least one distinguished writer to recommend that therapists make at least one positive, optimistic comment at the first meeting (Bruch, 1974, p. 3).

There is substantial evidence that the assessment process and the "helping" process are indivisible. For example, according to Carkhuff and Berenson (1967), "a meaningful diagnostic process flows out of an ongoing interactional process between therapist and client. There is no separate and distinct diagnostic process [p. 235]." Maier (1978) has written that "assessment and intervention . . . involve a range of continuously interwoven processes. Assessment activities are intimately intertwined with all transactions of helping, including a sense of urgency to initiate activities which may lead to change [p. 210]." Finally, one of the case histories presented in Standal and Corsini's classic, *Critical incidents in psychotherapy* (1959), describes a therapist, who, in one of the first two visits while "obtaining an anamnesis [p. 192]," unknowingly gave a client with marital difficulties absolution from a five and one-half year old post-hypnotic command. This incident is remarkable because the absolution occurred before the therapist thought therapy had begun:

> On the third interview, she came accompanied by her husband and her four-year-old son. She was in excellent spirits and reported a reconciliation. The obsessions and compulsions had gone, thanks to my treatment! When the interview was concluded, and I walked with her to the reception room, her hus-

band enthusiastically shook my hand, remarking on the wonderful things that doctors and psychiatrists can accomplish.

She never returned for any subsequent interviews, and I was left wondering "about the wonderful things psychiatrists accomplish." It seemed evident that I had done something "wonderful" and had alleviated her obsessive-compulsive psychoneurosis; but what was it?

I studied my careful anamnestic notes to try to find the answer [pp. 192–193].

When you assess a client, you cannot avoid changing that person simultaneously. A law of quantum mechanics, the Heisenberg Uncertainty Principle, provides an instructive parallel. Briefly stated, the principle is that the measurement of one of two related qualities of a particle (e.g., position and movement) produces change in the other. Any measurement on a system is said to "perturb" it. In specifying an object's movement, its position must be altered; in specifying position, its movement is changed.

Attempting to observe the particle has knocked it off its course, and the more accurately we observe its position the more uncertain we are to how much its velocity has been disturbed. Observation means interference with what we are observing. . . . Observation disturbs reality [Andrade, 1956, pp. 254–255].

This principle may apply to psychological measurement as well. It seems likely that a client's ongoing psychological development (i.e., "movement") must be altered to measure or assess that person's diagnosis or mental status—his or her psychological "position." Once, a woman made an appointment with me over the telephone immediately after her husband said he would leave her if she did not "get into therapy." After making the appointment, she asked, "So can I tell my husband I'm 'in therapy' now?" The woman later told me that she did tell her husband of her forthcoming meeting with me and that her relationship with him then began to change. Any contact with a therapist changes a client's circumstances in one way or another.

Even though it would be simpler if it were not so, you likely begin to influence a client's "movement" as soon as you begin to learn about "position." This is apt to be true even if you intend to reserve the first meeting(s) for diagnosis, assessment, and treatment planning. If assessment does not produce improvement, it will produce deterioration.

Failure to appreciate this can harm clients in a number of ways. For example, in a setting—usually a clinic or institution—where the intake is done by someone other than the therapist, some clients experience the assignment of a therapist as a rejection from the intake worker, even if procedures are explained carefully. Many people are known to deteriorate precipitously immediately after hospitalization, and this "rejection" may be one of the causes. Also, the recommendation of either hospitalization or therapy may be viewed as a vote of "no confidence."

Your failure to recognize the relationship between assessment and counseling may be harmful to clients who are very self-disclosing during the first or second meeting. A number of times, people have shared a great deal with me during an early session and, much to my dismay, did not return for further visits. I believe now that this happened because I was learning so much so quickly that I failed to provide, when they were most needed, the necessary helper characteristics described in chapter 1. A client can say "too much" in an early meeting and feel exposed or embarrassed in a setting not yet known to be safe. You can help such people by suggesting that they "slow down a bit," knowing that this may help avert a feeling of panic after the meeting is over. Sometimes it is best to be "therapeutic" from the very beginning at the expense of a prompt assessment.

DIAGNOSIS AND HELPING

Diagnosis probably is the component of the assessment process that does the most damage. Although the terms "diagnosis" and "assessment" have been used interchangeably to this point, the two are far from synonymous. It is possible to assess mental status, formulate a treatment plan, and write a rich, accurate description of a person without a diagnosis. (Indeed, the various diagnostic terms—before they were assigned an importance unto themselves—originally were meant to be shorthand summaries of such descriptions.) Conversely, it is possible to diagnose in lieu of understanding.

Although classification systems have the potential to be beneficial to clients, clinicians, and researchers, it is clear that our abuse of such systems has interfered with the effective therapy of countless individuals. It must be emphasized that our *use* of whatever terms are popular at the time has done the damage—not the terms themselves. After all, they are only words. Nonetheless, there is little doubt that the assignment of words and terms such as dyslexia, hyperactive, sexual dysfunction, MBD, ego-dystonic homosexuality, borderline, and developmental reading disorder often interferes with helping. Such terms (and dozens of similar ones) have come to imply that the client has a discrete difficulty readily identifiable as outside the range of typical functioning. The plain truth is that we do not know this to be the case. Moreover, even though a diagnosis may be made at a very transient, atypical moment in a client's life, many treat these diagnoses as permanent. They often are recorded and haunt people for years.

There is little doubt that therapists and counselors are shunned by many because they fear these implications of being diagnosed or declared as having a mental disorder or illness. As outlined in chapters 1 and 2, effective counseling must be based on a foundation of optimism and mutual respect. It is apt to be short-term—quickly identifying and utilizing the client's strengths and goals. It is hard to imagine such work occurring when words that we have allowed to become pejorative and dehumanizing are put by us in the forefront. Again, it is not the words that are the problem. The obstacle is our careless use of them, which has led the public and many professionals to treat them with an undeserved reliability and validity. Parenthetically, it probably complicates matters even more if you avoid such terms when talking with clients but use the terms freely in your written notes and discussions with colleagues. Such dissemblance may result in the client's secret fear that "My doctor thinks I'm crazy but won't tell me."

One of the merits of the DSM-III is that its authors seem well aware of the limits of DSM-III classifications. They write:

> It should be understood, however, that for most of the categories the diagnostic criteria are based on clinical judgment, and have not yet been fully validated by data about such important correlates as clinical course, outcome, family history, and treatment response. Undoubtedly, with further study the criteria for many of the categories will be revised. . . . Thus, this final version of DSM-III is only one still frame in the ongoing process of attempting to better understand mental disorders [American Psychiatric Association, 1980, pp. 8, 12].

Cousins (1979) has struck a responsive chord in pointing out the dangers of diagnosis. In 1954, he was told that he had a serious heart condition and that strenuous exercise would be fatal. He refused to accept the diagnosis, exercised vigorously shortly thereafter, and has been exercising regularly ever since. Paul Dudley White, the famous heart specialist, later told Cousins that if he "accepted the verdict of the specialists in 1954, [he, Cousins] probably would have confirmed it [Cousins, 1979, p. 158]." Cousins has written that White's support of his decision to reject the specialist's diagnosis gave him confidence in his rapport with his body.

Cousins (1979) writes the following regarding his dramatic successful recovery from yet another life-threatening disease:

> It all began, I said, when I decided that some experts don't really know enough to make a pronouncement of doom on a human being. And, I said I hoped they would be careful about what they said to others; they might be believed and that would be the beginning of the end [p. 160].

These inspiring comments of Cousins and White are all the more noteworthy because they regard *physical* disorders, which, for the most part, are diagnosed with more reliability and validity than mental disorders. Moreover, only rarely is there stigma associated with a physical disorder.

With psychological disorders, terms that originally were meant to describe a cluster of behaviors and ease communications among professionals gradually became entities unto themselves. The nature and dangers of this insidious process, which can victimize adults as well as children, are described by Ross (1980):

> A child behaves in a certain manner, and the people with whom that child interacts consider that behavior to be a problem. There are other children who behave in the same or similar manner, and eventually such a group of children comes to the attention of a specialized profession, say psychologists. These psychologists, in order to be able to communicate with one another, decide to give the problematic behavior of that group of children a distinctive label. Let us say they call it *odium* (a word of Latin origin which describes behavior that arouses disapproval and condemnation). There is, of course, no such psychological disorder; we use it as a fictitious example of what can happen after a label has been invented out of the need for a convenient description of some children's behavior.
>
> Before long, people tend to forget that originally the word was meant to identify behavior and the children whose behavior occasioned the invention of the label will now be said to *have* odium. The word has become a thing; the concept has been reified. What usually happens next is that what started out as a label becomes an explanation. People who ask why these children behave that way will be told, "Because they have odium." Obviously, nothing has been explained. After this, it will not be long before the noun, which has been used as a label for a cluster of behaviors, comes to be used as an adjective in describing children who engage in these behaviors. One now speaks of an odious child, and children, thus labeled, will see themselves in that, usually uncomplimentary light. In fact, such children will now explain their own behavior in terms of the label: "I can't help behaving that way, for I am an odious child." Furthermore, since people expect odious children to behave in a certain characteristic fashion, children so labeled often live up to these expectations, especially if "odious children" are segregated in schools and institutions where people expect them to behave the way odious children do [p. 14]*

Some clients ask for a diagnosis in an early session, apparently believing that it will help them understand themselves. When a client asks a question such as, "Tell me, Doc, am I crazy?" or, "Am I manic-depressive?" you will facilitate treatment by discussing and commenting on the reliability and validity of diagnostic classifications. Your failure to do so sustains the process described by Ross.

There is widespread evidence that, with these and other clients, diagnosis may interfere with effective counseling unless you ensure that it does not. As the following passage implies, those who prepared the DSM-III are aware of this danger:

A common misconception is that a classification of mental disorders classifies individuals, when actually what are being classified are disorders that individuals have. For this reason, the text of DSM-III avoids the use of such phrases as "a schizophrenic" or "an alcoholic," and instead uses the more accurate, but admittedly more wordy "an individual with Schizophrenia" or "an individual with Alcohol Dependence" [American Psychiatric Association, 1980, p. 6].

Predictably, children and minority groups seem to be hurt most by current diagnostic procedures. Carroll and Reppucci (1978), for example, studied the relative meanings among professionals of three clinical classifications for children—mentally retarded, emotionally disturbed, and juvenile delinquent. Forty grade 6–9 teachers and 32 mental health workers were asked questions regarding expectations for success in school, treatment strategies, and motivation to work with children of each classification. All 72 participants in the study confidently made these judgments with no information other than the classification. The three diagnoses conveyed distinct meanings which differed significantly, in a consistent fashion, across the two professional groups.

Foster and Keech (1977) found that expectations of teachers toward children diagnosed "educable mentally retarded" negatively biased the teachers' interpretation of videotaped behavior of these children. The authors concluded that such categorization limits the effectiveness of services offered and that noncategorical educational programs are needed.

An inevitable consequence of professionals' careless, and sometimes thoughtless, use of diagnostic terms is that others have followed suit. For example, Gibbons, Sawin, and Gibbons (1979) found that 80 college students rated identical interview transcripts significantly differently depending on whether or not the person interviewed was described as "retarded." The students developed a patronizing attitude toward the "retarded" person, for whom they predicted less future success. Cohen (1978) found that average and high self-esteem ex-offenders and former mental patients approached a job interview with enhanced self-esteem if they knew that the interviewer did not know of their previous classification.

Moreover, many have concluded that the use of diagnostic terms often interferes with therapy and counseling. Schofield (1964) and Davis (1976) are two of many who have pointed out the subjective nature of diagnosis and the need to respond to each person as unique, regardless of diagnosis or apparent similarity. The recent finding that overdiagnosis of pathology in Chicanos often results in their inappropriate exclusion from therapy (Roll, Miller, & Martinez, 1980) supports the conclusions of these writers.

Ross (1980) has commented on the "arbitrary and relative nature of the definition of psychological disorders [p. 20]." In fact, he suggests that "we must classify not behavior but people's judgments about behavior [p. 15]."

Along these lines, although the reliability of the DSM-III classifications is generally higher than that of DSM-II, there is room for improvement. In the DSM-III, the reliability of the adolescent and child classifications is described as "only fair [American Psychiatric Association, 1980, p. 469]," and "the reliability of the assessment of severity of psychological stressors is at least fair [p. 469]." The final, overall reliability coefficient for Axis I (all mental disorders except personality disorders and specific development disorders) is 0.52 for children and adolescents and 0.72 for adults.

There is little or no evidence that diagnostic assessment is helping to point the way to effective treatment. Indeed, as described above, such procedures may interfere with treatment. Along these lines, Crocetti, Spiro, and Siassi (1980) presented 30 psychiatrists in private practice and 38 clinicians from a community mental health center four case descriptions and asked for treatment recommendations. Based on the results, the authors question whether "diagnostic classifications are to continue to have any value or meaning [p. 213]." The performance of the 68 experienced workers was described as "woefully poor [p. 213]." It is problem formulation that is necessary for effective treatment, not diagnosis (Strupp, 1978b).

When diagnostic terms are used with sensitivity, or avoided altogether, the client may reap the benefits. This is pointed out by Weinberg (1977) regarding the word "alcoholic," but the principle would seem to apply to any of a number of terms:

> The greatest advantage of dropping the label "alcoholic" is the elimination of the strongest point of resistance for a large proportion of clients. Many will eventually concede everything else—that alcohol use produces harmful results and cannot be successfully controlled—but will not admit to being alcoholics. What the client is really saying, of course, is "I am not a bad person." Why, then, argue over a word? . . . I simply model disinterest in the label and minimize discussion of it. . . . My whole thrust is to attend to the relevant issue, which is not a label or a word, but harmful and uncontrollable consequences of drinking [p. 255].

Other popular terms are found wanting when they are examined closely. For example, Applebaum (1979) has commented on the recent, almost faddish, use of the term "borderline," which has been shown to have a broad range of meanings, depending on who is using it. Similarly, the World Federation of Neurology has defined "specific developmental dyslexia" as:

> A disorder manifested by difficulty in learning to read despite conventional instruction, adequate intelligence, and sociocultural opportunity. It is dependent upon fundamental cognitive disabilities which are frequently of constitutional origin [Rutter, 1978, p. 12].

Examination of this definition has led Eisenberg (1978), a noted expert in the field of learning, to conclude, "In the face of logical analysis, the entire concept collapses so totally that one begins to wonder just how a distinguished group of neurologists came to agree on a non-definition of a non-entity [p. 31]."

Finally, another problem is that the various classifications of mental disorders are thought by some to be highly dependent on culture, political considerations, and social custom (Scheff, 1975; Szasz, 1961; Waxler, 1977). This conclusion is to be expected, since even physical disorders have been found to vary greatly in severity and prevalence depending on "geographical area, the time, the social customs, the occupation. . . . The environment is often as important as the microbe in the determination of microbial disease [Dubos, 1959, pp. 93, 98]."

In summary, even the most sophisticated and promising diagnostic classification system is subjective, has been shown to interfere with treatment, and has been misunderstood and applied inappropriately by a broad range of professionals and others. Thus, it stands to reason that many (e.g., Garmezy, 1978; Ross, 1974; Schain, 1977; Werry, 1972) have called for restraint and compassion in the use of diagnostic terms.

Indeed, if we do not restrict ourselves, we will be restricted by others. For example, the California Department of Education recently has been forbidden to use any standardized intelligence tests to identify black children as being "educable mentally retarded." In a scathing indictment of assessment procedures, Judge Robert Peckham concluded that "validation has been assumed, not established, for blacks [Plotkin, 1980, p. 12]."

Schacht and Nathan (1977, p. 1017) have stated that our "equivalent of the Copernican revolution" will be needed before significant change is made in our diagnostic procedures. However, as the variety of examples below indicates, we may not have to wait that long—the revolution is in progress.

THE CLIENT'S STRENGTHS

According to the Heisenberg Uncertainty Principle, measurement of a particle's position will either speed up or slow down its movement. As clarified above, typical assessment procedures are likely to interfere with the client's development. It is of supreme importance that—beginning with the first meeting—you assess clients in such a way that they are reintroduced to their strengths—not their weaknesses. We have a responsibility to accelerate growth, not retard it. Exploration of difficulties and problems is needed; but early, excessive attention to imperfections may begin counseling on a discouraging note that can take weeks or months to overcome—if the client persists.

There are many ways that you can help each client recapture self-confidence, optimism, and independence. For example, many clients enter therapy feeling discouraged and unable to cope. Such people are apt to see their decision to see you as an admission of weakness. With such individuals, when the opportunity presents itself, I have found it useful to help them view this decision as a sign of strength. My failure to do so would be tacit agreement with their discouraging prejudice. It is a sad comment that many of us have allowed a decision that typically reflects courage and self-determination to be viewed by many as an admission of weakness and failure.

Along these lines, some clients believe that it is "wrong" to feel certain ways. These people often use the term "negative emotion" to describe, for example, anger, depression, or jealousy. Some will experience immediate, visible relief when you tell them that such feelings are not intrinsically bad and that these emotions, like others they are more comfortable with, may be within the range of typical human functioning.

Another burden sometimes placed on clientele is the use of the word "patient" or, even worse, "my patient." Regardless of the dictionary used, this word connotes a sick or disordered person who is under someone's care, a passive recipient of a treatment of some kind. It is an understatement to say that this term fails to describe those involved in an effective, helping relationship. If you use the word "patient," you should examine your motivation for doing so. For, as noted above, encouragement is a necessary ingredient in effective therapy, and few will find it encouraging when you imply that they are sick. (It should be mentioned that these comments are not directed toward psychiatrists. A growing number of psychiatrists rarely use the word "patient," but I know a number of psychologists, counselors, and social workers who do.)

Dingman (1980) prefers the terms "customer" or "patron." Others prefer the word "client." If none of these seems right for you, you may find that no special word is needed. For example, some speak of the "people," "students," or "individuals" they are "working with" or "seeing" in therapy or counseling. The point to be remembered is that what you call a person who seeks your professional help will influence that person's self-perception. Growth is apt to be slowed down if you unnecessarily place an individual's problem in the context of sickness or illness; growth is apt to be accelerated if you help the person view his or her situation more positively.

In addition, any atypical behavior, no matter how bizarre, disconcerting, or puzzling, can be viewed as a positive attempt to cope. For example, what some view as mental illness, others view as a "healthy" attempt to cope under stress (Bloch, 1978; Glasser, 1977). Cameron (1963) points out that even delusions and hallucinations, typically thought of as indications of severe disorder, are best viewed as "signs that a patient is actively trying to cope . . . that he is actually trying to get well [p. 618].'' Helping a client identify what a disturbing behavior is intended to *accomplish* is the first step toward finding more satisfactory ways of achieving that goal.

The new multiaxial evaluation system presented in the DSM-III reflects a growing recognition of the importance of identifying client strengths. Axis V, Highest level of adaptive functioning past year, is now included ''because usually an individual returns to his or her previous level of adaptive functioning after an episode of illness [American Psychiatric Association, 1980, p. 28].'' There are a number of other reasons to identify client strengths, and the Axis V framework for doing so seems quite good. Although Axis V is not part of the ''official diagnostic assessment [p. 23],'' it may turn out that Axis V is the most important one of all.

There are a number of other ways to identify and utilize client strengths in counseling that seem very promising. For example, Dinoff, Rickard, Love, and Elder (1978) found that emotionally disturbed children benefit from a sharing of detailed knowledge of both case materials and treatment techniques. The sharing resulted in an increase in client involvement in treatment and a reduction in unnecessary professional secrecy. Along similar lines, Ryle (1979) reports an encouraging approach to short-term counseling in which the client and counselor share hypotheses regarding therapeutic goals, treatment plan, and the success with which these are implemented and achieved.

Totman (1976) found that treatment of individuals with sleeping difficulties via placebo was significantly more successful for those who made decisions about their ''dosage.'' Armstrong and Booth (1979) report an obesity management program in which clients have atypical responsibility in treatment decisions. The counselor remained in the background while the clients were ''managers of their own maladaptive eating behaviors [p. 286].'' Weight loss results were ''comparable to the best results in the literature [p. 286].'' Finally, Kirsch (1978) reports a successful case study of a 28-year-old woman who developed and implemented her own behavior therapy program. She assumed the ''dual role of client and therapist while the therapist [assumed] the role of supervisor [p. 302].'' Thus, a wide range of clients, if given the opportunity, seem to have limitless capacity to draw upon their psychological resources and make decisions that help themselves in therapy.

Another decision—often reserved for the therapist—that clients seem entirely capable of making is whether or not to participate in a group. There seem to be as many theories as there are group therapists regarding which types of clients are most suited for group work. Yet, self-selection may be best.

For example, Corey, Corey, and Callanan (1979) recommend that a client make the decision after attending about two group sessions.

In this way, leaders encourage a process of self-selection that gives members the responsibility of deciding what is right for them. Actually, experiencing the group for a time enables them to make an informed decision about participation [p. 163].

Eric Berne (1961) also discourages professional screening, viewing it as a sign of professional inadequacy. He states, "In general, the behavior of a patient in a group cannot be reliably predicted from his behavior in daily life or in individual interviews [p. 169]."

As with individual counseling, clients, once in a group, can quickly draw upon their strengths if we permit them. Yalom (1975), a widely-recognized expert on group processes, advocates regularly scheduled leaderless group meetings as an adjunct to traditional, therapist-led groups. He has found that this lessens dependency and fosters autonomy and responsibility among group members. Anderson (1978), in a study using 80 college students, found a self-directed group to be more helpful than either a therapist-led Rogerian or a therapist-led Gestalt group; criteria used were intermember empathy, group cohesiveness, feelings of alienation, and sense of autonomy. Anderson concluded that "the lack of a leader is assumed to enhance members' freedom [p. 89]."

Otteson (1979) obtained similar results using 36 "chronic male schizophrenics [p. 649]." Here, a buddy-oriented, leaderless group was significantly more effective than a traditionally led group or a no-treatment control group, as measured by discharge or recidivism rate. Finally, a thorough survey of a broad range of consciousness-raising groups—groups without professional leaders—led Warren (1976) to conclude that these groups have much in common with traditional psychotherapeutic groups in both process and outcome. A wide range of clients have demonstrated more of an ability to help themselves and others than some would care to admit. This seems especially true in groups, which allow considerable opportunity for reality testing (Brandes, 1977), social affiliation, and learning (Galanter, 1978; Sidel, 1975).

In summary, you can be a source of help only to the extent that you look for strengths and avoid premature, disparaging, inappropriate classification. Also, it is necessary that you avoid any related, demeaning procedures, questions, or routines (Bruch, 1974; Rogers, 1970; Wachtel, 1980). Our classifications may prove helpful someday. Until they do, they should be used with sensitivity and restraint. Assessment should reflect your belief that the client has a dignity equal to your own (Erikson, 1973). "Facilitate ordinary developmental processes [Maier, 1978, p. 195];" do not hinder them. Clients—whether adults or children—have remarkable self-curative forces (Karenza, 1978; Padow, 1977-78; Schofield, 1964). Allow them to emerge.

A number of years ago, a guidance counselor asked me what a "latent homosexual" was. She went on to tell me about a high-school sophomore who, when he was four years old, was seen hugging another young boy at nursery school. Their teacher at the time wrote in each boy's record that he was a "latent homosexual." This comment made its way into each boy's cumulative record and remorselessly followed them through school, year after year, for 12 years. The "diagnosis" was read by a number of people over the years and proved to be a source of misery to each boy and their families. Ancillary workers have mimicked our bad habits in the use of classifications, which they will use with responsibility only after we do.

The assessment process is your first opportunity to reintroduce the client to his or her strengths. If this opportunity is missed, effective therapy is not likely to follow.

Chapter 4
Easily Observable Physical Characteristics: Age, Gender, and Skin Color

'Tis but a part we see, and not a whole.
> —Alexander Pope, Essay on Man,
> Epistle i, line 60

The ideal would be the situation where individual
characteristics of the therapist instead of gender
and such other attributes as race, age, and social
class would determine the appropriate therapist-client
match in each case.
> —Hannah Lerman, 1978, p. 250.

There is another way in which many of us fail to recognize strengths of clients. Some therapists and counselors draw conclusions regarding a person's suitability for treatment with them—or with anyone, for that matter—based on easily observable physical characteristics of the client. Such therapists typically assume, for example, that women are best treated by women, or that minority clients are best advised to see minority counselors. Such assumptions are superficial and untenable. As illustrated below, it has not been demonstrated that client–counselor physical similarity and therapeutic outcome are related. Regardless of your age, gender, or skin color, if you work, or intend to work, primarily with those who appear similar to yourself, you are apt to be making a mistake that will compromise your effectiveness with whomever you see. Such a stance is likely to deny your services to some who might benefit from them. And, it denies you the necessary personal expansion and enrichment that comes from interaction with a diverse range of individuals.

As a clinical psychology intern at the Illinois State Psychiatric Institute, the first client assigned to me—the first person I saw in psychotherapy—was a black woman who was hospitalized after two attempts to take her life. Although I was a good deal more shaky than she during our early sessions, our relationship developed into one gratifying to us both. She eventually said she would have killed herself if it had not been for me, and that may be true. During my internship year, in which, typically, I did not have many clients, I was assigned a youngster diagnosed as "catatonic schizophrenic," an Indian woman, and a 70-year-old man, informally described to me as "brain damaged and beyond help." I also led a "discharge group" (for individuals about to be discharged from the institution) of people whose age averaged about twice my own. I do not know if I was assigned such a broad range of clients intentionally or randomly. Whichever, I am grateful. My relationships with these clients accelerated my growth as a therapist and taught me, before I had a chance to learn otherwise, that my effectiveness was not related to clients' age, gender, or skin color. Ever since, I have gone out of my way to work with a visibly diverse range of clients.

Contrary to the opinion of many, I believe that you should bend over backwards to avoid stating or implying that you—or any other therapist—are best suited to work with any particular "group." And, even though words (e.g., "Black," "White," "elderly") are used in this chapter which imply that people can be classified accurately into such groups, that is not always the case. Many of the dangers of classification systems described in chapter 3 also apply to classification based on appearances. There are an infinite number of skin colors, and experts are yet to agree on a definition of "race." And, who is to say at what age one becomes "elderly," or at what one is too young or too old for counseling? And, regarding gender, a colleague tells the story of an intern she was supervising who was referred a woman with a very confused sexual identity. This client was referred after almost two years of therapy with a therapist with an excellent reputation. The client told the intern that she led this therapist, whom she disliked, to believe that she was a man. She wanted to see if she could "fool him," and that was the only reason she stayed in "therapy" with him for as long as she did. This story was confirmed when the former therapist sent the treatment summary to the intern, referring to the client throughout the report as "Mr." and "he"!

I do not believe that every therapist should try to be a generalist—equally helpful to all. But, to the extent that you do become specialized as a therapist, do so on the basis of your personality, the personality of each client, and the relationship that develops between you.

Although this chapter is addressed to counselor biases and preferences, a word should be said about those of the client. Some people will seek out or request to see a counselor visibly similar to themselves in some way. For example, a man may prefer a male counselor, or an elderly person may avoid a young counselor just out of graduate school. Whenever possible, I believe that this type of request should be granted. If it is, a client is much more apt to keep a first appointment (Ersner-Hershfield, Abramowitz, & Baren, 1979). Also, it is better that a person in need see a therapist than not see a therapist, regardless of the reasons. Along these lines, you should do all you can to assure that the professional staff you work with and those you refer people to are as diverse as possible along these easily observable dimensions so that you can grant the variety of client requests that might be made.

In the early meetings with a client who has chosen you because of your appearance, it is important that you discuss this choice. A person who chooses a therapist in this way may be making other important, personal decisions in an equally superficial manner. Such judgments may be an unrecognized source of frustration and may be related to the difficulties that have led the client to you. If the choice goes unexamined, you support the underlying prejudicial thinking.

Unusually specific requests are the most likely to be clues to important psychological processes. A man once made an appointment with me only after ascertaining from the secretary that I was married, but had no children at the time. He was having marital problems, not the least of which was a serious disagreement with his wife regarding whether or not they should try to have a child. The man's unexpressed anger toward his wife had intruded into his relationship with other women and was jeopardizing his job, where his immediate supervisor happened to be a woman. He was sure that only a married man without a child could understand him. We discussed this belief, and, as a result, he became much more candid with his wife. After three visits with me, he reported much more satisfactory communication between him and his wife, his work situation stabilized, and he stopped coming to see me. I believe that if I had failed to discuss this man's request to see me, therapy would have lasted much longer and would have been less effective.

This story also underscores the importance of working closely with anyone (e.g., a secretary or receptionist) who makes appointments for you. Clients occasionally volunteer important information to such individuals that they may not mention to you. With certain individuals, your effectiveness as a therapist will depend upon the extent to which coworkers are accustomed to sharing with you anything out of the ordinary that the client tells them.

Some people, dissatisfied with the progress they are making with you, may request that you refer them to a therapist of a certain age, gender, or skin color (e.g., "Dr. Brenner, I think I would like to see a woman counselor," "Dr. Brenner, I would like to see a black counselor," or "You're too old. You remind me of my father. Can you refer me to a younger counselor?"). When such a request occurs, I feel obligated to make the best possible referral, granting the client's request. Otherwise, a person in need may discontinue treatment and avoid such relationships in the future. However, I always encourage the client to examine the request, asking questions like, "How will it help you to see a woman?" or "How will it help you to see a younger (or older) therapist?" One thing leads to another in such conversations, and, as often as not, realizing that there is "nothing to lose," a client will disclose something that has been withheld for fear that I would not or could not understand. At this moment, if the counselor evidences the empathy and composure described in chapter 1, the client is likely to set aside, gradually, the wish to see a different therapist.

I believe that many professionals irresponsibly have led the public and impressionable, younger colleagues to believe that a therapist who is visibly similar to a client is apt to be more helpful than one who is not. As clarified below, this opinion is confirmed by neither published studies nor clinical practice. It sounds reasonable that similar appearance between client and counselor connotes similar life experiences, which, in turn, make an empathic relationship more likely. But, this has not been shown to be the case. Yet, it is likely that many people who may benefit from therapy are avoiding it because a counselor of, say, the "right" gender is not available. The example we set is crucial. Clients, by and large, will believe that physical characteristics are an important ingredient in psychotherapy to the degree that counselors do. It is important that we demonstrate that physical appearance is not a barrier to effective communication.

There are anecdotal and published reports that say, for example, black counselors are more effective with black clients than with white, or that women are more likely to be helped by women counselors. And, some have concluded that therapeutic efforts are wasted on the very young and very old. However, for whatever reasons, some clinicians cite such reports disproportionately and seem blind to contradictory evidence. It cannot help to mislead the public. Each of us should do whatever possible to allow clients to find counselors in a considered, unprejudiced manner, in a climate free from politics, ideology, and misrepresentation.

Before discussing age, gender, and skin color, it should be pointed out that counselors, too, have been found to be willing to make judgments about clients based on virtually any observable characteristic. For example, Cook, Kunce, and Getsenger (1976) studied 80 counselors of differing effectiveness, as determined by ratings of supervisors. The counselors were asked to rank physically disabled clients along a number of personality measures. These disabled clients were, in fact, equivalent to nondisabled clients along these measures. The less effective counselors rated disabled and nondisabled clients significantly differently. The effective counselors rated the disabled clients as similar to nondisabled on the same measures.

Certain "hard to treat" clients (e.g., severely disturbed individuals, some who abuse alcohol or other drugs, those who behave in a bizarre manner) can be identified by their appearance. An examination of therapists' attitudes toward such clients led Giovacchini (1977) to conclude that they often undeservedly are designated as difficult-to-treat, or even "untreatable," by experienced workers wishing to avoid the challenge of working with them. Moreover, Giovacchini found that such clients often are assigned to less experienced workers, interns, residents, trainees, and volunteers who may be less able to help. Such assignments often make the "untreatable" designation come true. Failure to take on the range of clients that comes your way is apt to lead to your stagnation and diminished effectiveness with those people that you are willing to see.

Indeed, the reluctance of many to work with alcohol and heroin abusers has served to perpetuate certain myths about "addicts" and "alcoholics." For example, some workers now question the widespread belief that Alcoholics Anonymous (AA) alone is the "treatment of choice" for individuals who abuse alcohol (e.g., Corrigan, 1980; Curlee-Salisbury, 1977). In speaking of AA members, Curlee-Salisbury writes, "although some members (often, unfortunately, very vocal ones) insist that 'only an alcoholic can help an alcoholic,' an increasing number consider it desirable to utilize every type of help available. . . . An increasing number of persons affiliated with the organization have come to see the usefulness of other treatment modalities [p. 271]."

Similarly, in a study of 253 heroin abusers (Longwell, Miller, & Nichols, 1978), using urinalysis for heroin as the outcome measure, no difference was found in the effectiveness of exaddict and nonaddict counselors. Both groups were found to be significantly more effective than no counselor. Therapists who encourage drug abusers to work exclusively with former abusers may avoid some trying sessions and some late–night telephone calls, but they may not always be acting in the clients' best interest.

Finally, treatment assumptions regarding yet another recognizable group —intellectually deficient individuals—may also be invalid. Hayes (1977), in one of the few such investigations available, studied twenty 5 to 15-year-old mild to borderline retarded individuals and 20 other individuals in the middle range of intellectual functioning. Hayes found the former group to be at least as responsive to psychotherapy as the latter, concluding:

> There are mentally retarded children who can benefit from psychoanalytic psychotherapy to the same extent, with the same length of treatment, as children of higher intelligence with similar psychological problems. These findings directly contradict the indiscriminate presumption that psychotherapy is inappropriate for the treatment of all mentally retarded persons [p. 150].

Next I will discuss the easily observable physical characteristics of clients about which therapists and counselors seem to have the strongest preferences and prejudices. These are age, gender, and skin color. I will emphasize the client–counselor combinations that have been given the most attention. Thus, for example, the discussion of "gender" will consider primarily whether women are served better by women therapists. The section on skin color will emphasize the black client–white counselor combination.

AGE

In a survey of psychologists, psychiatrists, and social workers, Schofield (1964) found that those in each professional group considered the "ideal patient" to be between 20 and 40 years old. This preference has remained stable (Steiner, 1978), with numerous surveys yielding similar results. Ironically, most therapists prefer to work with Schofield's so-called YAVIS clients (young, attractive, verbal, intelligent, successful)—those who would seem least in need of our help. I will present very little speculation here regarding *why* some therapists prefer to work with clients of a certain age or appearance. This is a personal question, which each therapist must answer in a personal way. Broad generalizations are not likely to help. Allport's 1954 classic, *The Nature of Prejudice*, is the best place to start if you wish to read explanations of why some people judge and draw conclusions about others without adequate information.

It is tempting to speculate why at least some counselors wish to avoid very young and elderly clients. These times in a person's life often are characterized by crucial struggles and tensions and lack the stability and equilibrium sometimes found in young and middle-adulthood. Moreover, there is something especially tragic about, say, a four-year-old with abusive parents, or with a severe physical or emotional problem. It can be equally trying to work with an elderly person with a life-threatening illness, a dying spouse, or gross physical or psychological deterioration. It is tempting, therefore, to say that such people are not likely to benefit from counseling or that someone else—a specialist, perhaps—should try to help.

Nonetheless, this position is unsupportable. When given the opportunity, individuals at the extremes of the age continuum have demonstrated a remarkable resiliency and potential to benefit from a therapeutic relationship. Yet, the mental health needs of neither children nor the elderly are being met (Blazer & Williams, 1980; Storandt, 1978; Wohlford, 1979).

Circumstances are so gloomy for children that Riscalla (1980) has concluded that even those professionals who appear to make an effort to help often abuse them unintentionally. One such form of abuse is the prescription of certain medications which are known to mask relevant symptoms and leave the child unimproved after they are discontinued. Invasion of privacy and denial of a right to legal counsel are also common, and, like Giovacchini (1977), Riscalla considers the assignment of inexperienced helpers to difficult clients inexcusable. She adds that such abuses will not be alleviated by more money, services, programs, and specialists. "The abuse of children by professionals and the prevention of this abuse depends on human qualities, and what is done for children on paper or in action is a by-product of those qualities [p. 73]."

As noted above, when given the opportunity, youngsters do remarkably well in treatment. For example, Bruch (1974) describes a six-year-old boy, almost mute, whom she treated with "serious courtesy" from the moment they met. She introduced herself, asked his name, told him what she knew of him and how she planned to help. Eventually, he responded very well to her in psychotherapy. When she asked him why he was so much more responsive to her than to his teachers in school, he answered, "The way you talk; I knew you knew I wasn't dumb [p. 8]."

Chronological age cannot be used as a reliable predictor of therapeutic responsiveness; every child has a unique developmental schedule which must be considered when determining suitability for counseling (Maier, 1978). Fenichel (1945) also advocates working with very young children. For example, regarding the removal of undesirable inhibitions, he states that:

Children's analyses are often more promising than those of adults, since the neurosis is still less incorporated and reassurances may still powerfully accelerate the analysis; children's analyses may also be of great prophylactic value, contrasted with analyses of adults [p. 576].

Another psychoanalyst (Bloch, 1978) has written a delightful, inspiring book of case studies of children she has treated. The youngest child she worked with began treatment at two and one half years of age, and some had their analyses completed by age five.

Both children and adolescents have responded successfully to a broad range of techniques. For example, Phillips and Grover (1979) concluded from their assertiveness training work with clients ranging in age from 11 to 17 that assertiveness training is "of inestimable value in the treatment of children [p. 171]." Croghan and Frutiger (1977) concluded that a contracting approach can be very successful with 6 to 12 year-olds with problems such as bedwetting and withdrawal. The authors have used this approach with a number of children, and specimen contracts are included in their article. Wallick (1979) reports successful treatment of a five-month-old girl with a reciprocal inhibition desensitization program. A two-year follow-up indicated that therapeutic gains were maintained.

Despite current practices, the elderly, too, prove very responsive to therapeutic intervention when given the opportunity. However, very few therapists are willing to work with the elderly. In a survey of 30 therapists in private practice, Weintraub and Aronson (1968) found that none was treating anyone over 60. Even though life expectancy has increased significantly since 1968—and promises to continue to do so—most therapists and counselors continue to avoid the elderly. But, Ingebretsen (1977), in a remark that sounds much like Maier's comment about children, noted that "age *per se* indicates nothing definite about the client's power or will to change [p. 319]." Fenichel (1945), too, advocates working with the elderly. He states that "several authors who have tried analyses with patients of very advanced age report considerable success [p. 576]."

Again, stereotypes prove to be inaccurate. Sviland (1978) describes a successful sex therapy service for the elderly directed toward helping those who wish to become more sexually liberated. Sviland concludes that we should provide "more such services to elderly couples and publicize their availability [p. 359]." Bruch (1974) writes of a successful therapeutic relationship with a 78 year-old woman who had been told by a number of therapists that "not much could be expected [from therapy] at her age [p. 9]." This woman told Bruch that "I felt you thought of me as somebody who could understand complicated things, and not just a wealthy old lady who wanted attention and needed pampering [p. 9]." Bruch writes, "the experience of my having talked openly about her problems, without any reference to her age, had encouraged her, and she insisted on continuing in therapy, with remarkably positive results [p. 9]."

The elderly can benefit from group as well as individual therapy. Deutsch and Kramer (1977) found that a significant number of more than 60 clients in five different groups made positive life changes directly attributable to the group experience. Most of the 60 had been depressed about either physical, mental, or social loss. The most frequent changes made as a result of the group were increased involvement with either volunteer or part-time work, and an increased ability to deal with life stresses. The authors also concluded that if these outpatient groups (or some equally effective treatment) had not been offered, many of the 60 people would have been institutionalized.

Those most familiar with the problems of the elderly discourage clinicians from specializing in this area. Smymer and Gatz (1979), for example, conclude that such specialization primarily would serve to segregate older adults. Kastenbaum (1978) also discourages "an all-out effort to cultivate a special field of geriatric psychotherapy," advocating instead examination of "the specific characteristics of the individual [p. 206]." By creating a separate specialty, he feels "We might, then, be contributing inadvertently to overemphasis on chronological age by cultivating this approach to psychotherapy [p. 205]."

There are at least three ways in which we might become more sensitive to the needs of young children and the elderly. First, avoid simple, traditional conclusions and decisions. For example, although many elderly people have physical problems, it is not necessarily helpful to alleviate those problems without a full understanding of the client. Removal of a symptom may also remove "the old person's explanation for what had gone wrong in his life [Kastenbaum, 1978, p. 214]." Regarding children, although conventional wisdom dictates that they be segregated in in-patient settings, Strauss, Downey, and Ware (1980) present a number of convincing arguments against such separation—even if this means increased contact with seriously disturbed adolescents.

Second, Gunn (1977) advocates the notion of partial mental incompetence for certain elderly people. The global view that dominates now, in which a person is judged competent for all purposes or incompetent on a similar basis, prevents those with partial mental incapabilities from living as full a life as they might. The same can be said for classifications such as "developmental delay" or "mental retardation" in young children. Many children so designated are placed in "special" classes or schools, even though they typically have certain skills superior to those of their "normal" age-mates.

Finally, with both the very young and the very old, be flexible. Roach and Maizler (1977) cite examples in which deviation from routine procedures can be helpful. For example, shorter, more casual meetings may be best for some clients. Greater therapist activity may be needed, as well as a gradual tapering off of visits as opposed to a relatively abrupt termination. With the elderly, therapy may have to be altered to suit one's physical problems. "Imagine trying to offer gentle reassurance to a hearing-impaired patient in a tone reserved for hailing a taxicab [p. 282]."

Further, your work with children and the elderly inevitably will enhance your understanding of the life-cycle and make you a more effective therapist for all clients, regardless of age (Ingebretsen, 1977). Kastenbaum's (1978) following comment regarding the elderly is equally valid for young children:

> The need for good research into the psychotherapeutic processes with elderly people is obvious—but even more evident is the need for more psychotherapy! In lieu of a substantial body of psychotherapy research with the elderly, at least it can be said that pessimism and nihilism have not been supported and that many types of theory and technique have yet to be applied systematically. Considering the impressive individual differences among elderly people and the broad range of psychotherapeutic approaches available, we have hardly begun to match treatment modality to the needs and strengths of the individual [p. 221].

If you are not working with at least a small number of people, say, less than eight or ten years of age, and others older than 65 or 70, ask yourself why not. The answer cannot be that the young and elderly are not good psychotherapy prospects, that it is in their best interest that you do not see them, or that your not seeing them is in the best interest of the clients that you do see. Develop intimate, caring relationships with the young and the old, and you will become a more complete, effective therapist for all. The young and the old lack social and political power. If the impetus for more effective care does not come from us, it will not come.

GENDER

Although opinions vary, many believe that women have suffered greatly from the bias and stereotyping of counselors and therapists. One does not have to look far for support of this conclusion. In 1959, Standal and Corsini's classic text, *Critical Incidents in Psychotherapy*, presented 23 actual case summaries (15 women and 8 men), each of which was included to illustrate a crucial turning point in treatment. Each case was presented by an anonymous therapist, and each was critiqued by a number of eminent therapists. All of the descriptions of the 15 women and their problems are sexist in some way. Here are just a few examples of the descriptions of the women:

> A girl of 27, very attractive . . . whose behavioral problem is sexual promiscuity [pp. 29, 35].

> From time to time her body would lean toward me and then lean away. My heart was beating like a triphammer [p. 40].

Her body seemed frail and limp with defeat. Instead of going to my chair, I touched her hand in a gesture of sympathy, whereupon she put her head against my stomach and clung to me [p. 66].

She was a good-looking patient [p. 116].

A very handsome statuesque young woman. I had noticed her several times and wondered about her. She had a pretty face and a figure good enough for the movies [p. 202].

In addition, sexual stereotypes seem to have played a role in the therapists' problem definition and case management. For example, in the description of a woman with a "promiscuous sex life . . . the therapist forbade her to behave that way in the future and threatened to hospitalize her if she did not act within socially acceptable bounds [pp. 246, 375]." One case is presented in which two women clients in a group fight for the attention of the male therapist, and another is presented in which a woman has a history of cunnilingus with a dog. Predictably, not one of the eight male clients was described as "handsome," had a transference-related problem with a woman therapist, or had a bizarre or "over-active" sexual life.

You may be thinking at this moment that the attitudes of the 23 anonymous therapists who wrote these summaries could not have been representative of those of informed clinicians at the time. However, among the experts who critiqued these cases were: Nathan Ackerman, Rudolph Dreikurs, Albert Ellis, Jerome Frank, Victor Frankl, Ernest Hilgard, J. McV. Hunt, O. Hobart Mowrer, Ruth Monroe, Carl Rogers, Frederick Thorne, Carl Whittaker, and Werner Wolff. And, not one of them raised any questions about the descriptions of these women.

These descriptions of women are representative of many appearing in books of that era. In Cameron's (1963) widely-read text, *Personality Development and Psychopathology: A Dynamic Approach*, the descriptions of girls and women are shocking. For example:

Boys see the objective world differently from the ways girls see it. . . . These differences are a function of basic differences in anatomy, physiology and private experience. . . . The urge to master, especially to master things beyond family life and family organizations, seems to be a masculine perspective everywhere. A narcissistic cathexis of the body and its adornment, and the pervasive interest in the care of children, seem to be feminine perspectives which transcend cultural and historical changes [p. 181].

Although women who evade the essentially feminine roles, and compete successfully with men, are usually praised for it, their choice is often the result of an inability to fulfill a woman's socially prescribed role, rather than a sign of superiority. [A woman] has powerful, inborn needs that cannot be satisfied in our culture unless she accepts the feminine roles of homemaker, wife and mother [p. 197].

And, there are current indications supporting the hypothesis that women continue to be stereotyped and misunderstood by many therapists, whose effectiveness consequently is impaired. For example, testimony and evidence regarding the proposed Mental Health Systems Act presented to a congressional subcommittee (Felipe-Russo, 1979) cited sex bias—against women—in the mental health delivery system. Also noted was the need for both more direct and more preventive services for women. Corrigan (1980) in a longitudinal study of 150 women with alcohol-related problems concluded that the popular stereotype of the "female alcoholic" is very inaccurate. The women in her study represented a very broad cross-section of age, residence, race, and socioeconomic status. Kwawer (1980) has arrived at similar conclusions regarding "female homosexuals."

Frey, Hetherington, and Glassman (1978) in a study of 100, first-time, mental institution admissions found that minor tranquilizers were prescribed to women significantly more often than men, regardless of diagnosis. And Donahue and Costar (1977) found the following in a study in which they presented, to 300 randomly selected high school guidance counselors, six case studies, half of which were described as male, half as female: "When the case study described a female, the counselors chose occupations that paid less, required less prerequisite education, and were more closely supervised than when the same case study described a male. Female counselors over 40 years of age exhibited the strongest tendency to do this [p. 481]."

At times, therapist bias can be quite varied. For example, Tanney and Birk (1976) concluded that both male and female counselors have biases toward women, sometimes viewing them excessively favorably and, sometimes, excessively unfavorably. Lowery and Higgins (1979), in another study in which a case description is presented to half the counselors as male and half as female, found that vocational counseling was recommended significantly more often for same-sex than for opposite-sex clients. The more experienced therapists rated women clients as less severely disturbed than male clients.

In the face of all this, it is hardly surprising that some (e.g., Glenn & Kunnes, 1973) advise that no woman should be in individual therapy with a male therapist unless she is in an all-female consciousness-raising group simultaneously, to counteract the harm done by the therapist. Others (e.g., Carter, 1971; Chesler, 1972; Kronsky, 1971; Rice & Rice, 1973) have concluded that therapists and clients should be matched by gender. Fitzgerald and Crites (1980), among others, advocate that courses on the special needs of women be included in the training of anyone who might do career counseling with women, an area that many think is particularly susceptible to harmful stereotyping. Finally, some advocate that there be separate principles for therapy and counseling with women (Oliver, 1978).

Notwithstanding the faults of past and present therapists and counselors, I believe it is a serious error when therapists primarily treat either men or women. First, there is little evidence that clients receive better care when they see a counselor of the same gender. Although one might assume that workers would be less apt to stereotype clients of their own gender, this has not been shown to be the case. For example, all of the studies referred to above in which women were stereotyped and misunderstood used both male and female counselors. And, some of the comments and descriptions in Standal and Corsini's text were written by women. Along these lines, men have been shown to be stereotyped, misunderstood, and ineffectively treated by both male and female counselors and researchers (Berman, 1979; Hill, Tanney, & Leonard, 1977; Parloff, Waskow, & Wolfe, 1978; Schaffer, 1980; Stokes, Fuehrer, & Childs, 1980; Toomer, 1978). It is sad but true that a number of both male and female counselors have been shown to misunderstand both men and women. "Neither same-sex nor opposite-sex pairing is a predictor of counseling process or outcome [Feldstein, 1979, p. 438]."

Movements toward matching clients and counselors by gender will exacerbate the deficiencies that exist. Separate principles for counseling men and women will do the same (Spiegel, 1979). Smith (1980) presents an extremely thorough, balanced review of both published and about-to-be–published work in the area of gender bias in counseling and psychotherapy. In it, she notes that many who have written on this topic have been committed to a certain point of view before initiating their research or therapy. She adds that the widely cited 1970 conclusion of Broverman, Broverman, Clarkson, Rosenkrantz and Vogel that "a double-standard of health exists for men and women [p. 5]" has been widely and undeservedly accepted, repeated, overgeneralized, and unquestioned by those wishing to believe it. Smith's conclusions are worth repeating:

Empirical support for the contention that counseling and psychotherapy are sexist and bad for women is extremely weak. Studies that demonstrate a bias of counselors against women or against nonstereotyped roles for women are balanced by an equal number of studies that showed the opposite condition that counselors have the same standards of mental health for women as they have for men, the same recommendations for jobs, educational plans, and personal decisions. They behave in nondiscriminatory ways; they express empathy and acceptance perhaps even in greater amounts for women than for men.

Contrasted with the prevailing view on counseling and clinical sex bias expressed in popular and professional literature, this conclusion seems surprising and radical. One can speculate on this contrast. Motivation to conduct research of this type was frequently ideological; that is, investigators seemed intent on establishing counselor sexism (a foregone conclusion in many minds). Designs were often weak. Small but statistically significant effects became sweeping, and categorical conclusions, widely disseminated. Research reviews on this topic tended to be selective. It can be demonstrated that studies showing a sex-bias effect have been cited more frequently than studies not showing that effect. Studies have been published more often when a sex-bias effect was shown, regardless of the quality of the study itself.

Stripped of the selectivity, motivation, and rhetoric, the body of evidence looks both different and more clear: Counselor sex bias has not been demonstrated despite a dozen years of attempts to do so [pp. 405–406].

In summary, strive to develop compassionate, empathic, therapeutic relationships with both men and women. As a helper, if you feel uncomfortable with or attracted toward either one or the other, try to find out why (Brodsky, 1977; Eisenbud, 1977; Hare-Mustin, 1977; Saretsky, 1977). Similarly, when you encounter a client who insists on seeing a male or female therapist, make the referral if necessary, but also try to help that person understand the request. Wilder, Hoyt, Zettle, and Hauck (1978) found that such individuals were less emotionally well-adjusted than those who did not care about the gender of the counselor they were about to see.

Sidney Jourard (1968) said the following when describing his efforts as a therapist to understand a client whose experience he could not duplicate:

But suppose a woman tells you, "My menstrual periods are agonizing. Can you understand how I feel?" Now I never menstruated . . . but I may have had experiences not unlike a period. A pain in my gut, or lower down; if I can acknowledge the breadth and depth of my own experiencing, I think my empathy has been enhanced and my chances of understanding and communicating my understanding are increased [p. 79].

Many people will come to you precisely because of the misery caused (at least in part) by biased, stereotyped judgments made by themselves and others. By example, you can help clients learn to relate to a broader spectrum of individuals. If you do not work to counteract superficial, inaccurate judgments, you encourage them.

SKIN COLOR

Current opinion and knowledge regarding therapist and client skin color is strikingly parallel to that regarding gender. Without question, there is evidence that white counselors have stereotyped and misunderstood non-white clients. Schmidt and Hancey (1979), for example, reviewed 500 case records and found an unrealistically optimistic bias in favor of middle- and upper-class clients, most of whom were white. The Roll et al. study (1980) reported in the previous chapter found white therapists to have a "misperception of Chicanos as a homogeneous group [p. 158]." Gynther and Green (1980), after reviewing 27 studies, report that the F, Sc, and Ma scales of the MMPI discriminate against blacks who are significantly more likely than whites to be identified falsely as deviant on the MMPI.

Fuller and Kern (1978) had confederate black and white clients act in a hostile manner in an interview with 20 white counselors. Ten counselors met with the black "client" and ten with the white. Using three different measures, including the Taylor Manifest Anxiety Scale, the white counselors were found to be significantly more anxious with the hostile black client than with the hostile white client. Since "composure" is a necessary trait of the effective therapist, it seems logical to conclude from this study that any black client who might ever express anger in therapy should not see a white therapist. Gale, Beck, and Springer (1978), in a study of 262 people seen at a psychiatric emergency unit, found race to be an accurate predictor of both diagnosis and disposition. Black women were asked to return for short-term therapy more than white women or men of any skin color. Finally, Fry, Kropf, and Coe (1980) in a study of 60 graduate-level black and white counselors, found that both the type and appropriateness of counselors' responses were best with the black-black and white–white dyads.

Such findings have led many to call for special services for minority clients (Buck, 1977; Carter, 1978). On the other hand, there are those who encourage clinicians to become more appreciative and understanding of the differences among ethnic groups and to use that knowledge in the treatment of a diverse range of clients. For example, Ahn Topin (1980) presents a very sensitive description of the ways in which the cultural background of Asian–Americans might influence their response to a non-Asian therapist. She concludes that Asian-Americans are more likely to benefit from individual than from group work and advocates that a counselor working with Asian–Americans understand Asian nonverbal cues, which differ from European. Lager and Zwerling (1980) discuss time orientation of individuals who live in a ghetto that is oriented toward present and short-term goals. The authors hypothesize, therefore, that short-term therapy might be more effective than long-term for these individuals. Similarly, Korchin (1980) notes that knowledge of the differences between ethnic groups is necessary for anyone doing research on this topic; otherwise, data are apt to be misinterpreted.

There is considerable evidence that client and counselor should work to understand each other rather than be matched by skin color. Encouraging results are obtained when this is attempted. Many researchers report that minority clients are viewed *more* favorably and receive *better* care than white clients from counselors. In a number of studies, blacks and Chicanos were rated either equal or superior to whites on a variety of personality measures (McGill, 1980; Merluzzi & Merluzzi, 1978; Pritchard & Rosenblatt, 1980; Touliatos & Lindholm, 1980). And, a review of both clinical work and published studies indicates that racial homogeneity is not necessary for effective therapy (Griffith, 1977; Jacobs, Charles, Jacobs, Weinstein, & Mann, 1972).

Parloff, Waskow, and Wolfe (1978), in a thoughtful and comprehensive review, much like Smith's on gender, found very few well-designed studies showing superiority of the black–black or white-white combination over the black-white combination. They also note the inclination for researchers in this area to conduct one-session analogue studies using college students (e.g. Fry, Kropf, & Coe, 1980; Fuller & Kern, 1978). The relevance of such research to actual psychotherapy and counseling remains moot. They conclude that the interactive effect of client and counselor race has "not been adequately tested [p. 273]."

Sue and Sue (1977) provide helpful, sensitive suggestions for the counselor working with a client from a different cultural group, concluding, "The ultimate success of counseling is very much dependent upon the counselor's flexibility in using techniques appropriate not only to the cultural group but the individual as well [p. 427]."

In 1957, Montague wrote, "Race is a concept which can apply only to populations. It cannot be applied to an individual, but only to a population of individuals . . . race is a statistical concept . . . a relative term [pp. 70, 71]." Clients will come to you one at a time, and there is little of relevance that you can determine from the client's skin color. And, as noted above, to the extent that relevant information can be ascertained, it can be used to enhance the counseling relationship. I agree with Jones and Seagull (1977) who advocate that you seize the opportunity to enter such relationships and use them as a model of how people of differing backgrounds learn to help and understand each other.

CONCLUSIONS

It is commonplace, almost fashionable, for therapists and counselors to reach conclusions about clients and potential clients based on their easily observable physical characteristics. Many believe that common physical appearance between therapist and client implies common life or cultural experiences which, in turn, make an empathic, compassionate relationship more likely. This belief *sounds* sensible, but it is insupportable, nonetheless.

Published studies and reports of counselors ranging from psychoanalytic to behavioristic fail to support the notion that physical similarity between therapist and client enhances the therapeutic relationships. Indeed, this approach would seem to encourage superficiality and stereotyping in relationships. It also leaves children and the elderly, who lack helpers that are superficiallly equivalent, abandoned and misunderstood. The elderly have been shown to be remarkably responsive to a wide range of interventions, and children are more than young weather vanes of marital discord.

Until evidence clearly indicates otherwise, it would be best if you do not draw conclusions about relationships with new or potential clients based on appearances. Encourage clients and colleagues, too, to enter relationships in an open, unbiased manner. Let the fate of your relationship with each client be determined by your personalities.

Everyone suffers when you make therapeutic decisions based on social, political, or ideological considerations. Prejudice and stereotyping will die more slowly if, in the name of client welfare, we advocate it.

Chapter 5
Psychoactive Drugs

Doctor. Not so sick, my lord,
As she is troubled with thick-coming fancies,
That keep her from rest,
Macbeth. Cure her of that.
Canst thou not minister to a mind diseas'd,
Pluck from the memory a rooted sorrow,
Raze out the written troubles of the brain,
And with some sweet oblivious antidote
Cleanse the stuff'd bosom of that perilous stuff
Which weighs upon the heart?
Doctor. Therein the patient
Must minister to himself.

—Shakespeare,
Macbeth. Act V. Scene 3.

The witch doctor succeeds for the same reason all the rest
of us succeed. Each patient carries his own doctor inside
him. They come to us not knowing that truth. We are at
our best when we give the doctor who resides within each
patient a chance to go to work.

—Albert Schweitzer,
cited in Cousins, 1979, p. 69.

Often, your effectiveness will depend upon whether or not you are well informed about psychoactive drugs and whether or not you recommend their
use. Psychoactive drugs are those that primarily affect mental functioning

and that are prescribed to alter an individual's mood or thought processes. The most common classes of these medications are: antipsychotics (e.g., Thorazine, Mellaril, Haldol), antidepressants (e.g., Elavil, Tofranil), mood stabilizers (e.g., lithium), antianxiety drugs (e.g., Librium, Valium), and stimulants (e.g., Benzadrine, Ritalin).

Many clients are apt to introduce questions or concerns about the use, abuse, effectiveness, or side effects of these drugs. Still others will rely on you to identify their concern or questions and to initiate appropriate discussion. In either instance, regardless of whether or not you are a physician, you have a responsibility to respond in an informed way. Following are some examples of the types of questions you might be asked. "Dr. Brenner, this is our third visit, and things seem to be getting worse. I'm feeling *so tense*. Do you think a tranquilizer would help?" "Dr. Brenner, my physician prescribed Valium to me before I started seeing you. Should I continue taking them while I'm in therapy?" "I've been told by the school psychologist that my son is 'hyperactive' and should be put on Ritalin immediately. Can you tell me something about it? Do you think it's a good idea?" "I've been told by my former therapist to stay on a very low dose of Thorazine so I won't ever have to go back to the hospital again. But I've just read a newspaper article about tardive dyskinesia, and it scared me. Can I get tardive dyskinesia from only 25 mg. a day of Thorazine? And, if I did get it, would it go away if I stopped taking the Thorazine?" "I feel *so miserable*. Our family doctor said she'll prescribe an antidepressant for me if you'll phone and say that's a good idea. Would you do that for me, *please*?"

Each of these questions, and countless others like them, raises complex issues regarding the effectiveness and risks of psychoactive drugs or about the relationship between them and psychotherapy. Responses to these questions that amount to "Yes," "No," or "I'm not a physician; I think you should talk it over with your physician," may be disappointing, discouraging, or off the mark. Similarly, if you reply with a reflective comment or an interpretation, the client may feel misunderstood, that you are avoiding a direct response, or that you lack certain or basic information that should be at your command. You have an obligation to know a certain amount about these medications, regardless of whether or not you are permitted by law to prescribe them. This is an enormous, complex responsibility, one that is tempting to avoid. The amount of information available on each of these drugs is overwhelming, and new, important studies are published monthly in a wide range of books and journals. Nonetheless, the effective counselor —psychiatrist or not—needs to keep abreast of this information via reading, workshops, and consultations with well-informed colleagues. This knowledge will make you better prepared to respond in a helpful way to the clients who associate psychological problems with illness and disease, with those who neither know nor care if you are a psychiatrist, and with those seeking chemical solutions for their discomfort.

At times, this knowledge will be crucial even when a client does not inquire about medication. For example, a client may be experiencing troublesome side effects from a drug being taken that was prescribed six months or a year ago, or even longer, by a physician that he or she is no longer seeing. Your knowledge that depression is a frequent side effect of Thorazine or that anorexia is a frequent side effect of another phenothiazine, trifluoperazine (Honigfeld & Howard, 1978), may make the difference between success and failure in the treatment of a client.

However, even if you know a great deal about these medications, avoid recommending their use whenever possible. Consider them only after the safer, more productive solutions to a client's distress have been explored. As illustrated below, these drugs interfere with both assessment and therapy. Also, they have numerous side effects, ranging from the transient and merely annoying, to those that are irreversible or even life-threatening. Moreover, even the most well established ones have not proven cost-effective when compared to psychotherapy, relaxation training, and the like. Increasingly, both medical and nonmedical therapists are encouraging clients to explore alternatives to psychoactive medication. Further, many psychiatrists now dislike being thought of as "pill pushers." Many also resent being greeted with anger and disappointment when they suggest something other than chemotherapy to either clients desperately seeking immediate relief or nonmedical colleagues who refer for medication those individuals who present the greatest therapeutic challenges. The temptation is great to medicate such clients—to invoke the power and mystery of these chemicals which seem to produce dramatic, if not predictable, changes. Nonetheless, this temptation almost always should be resisted.

Greater knowledge of these drugs will increase the confidence with which you prescribe them or, if you are a nonmedical therapist, with which you consult with a physician regarding a particular client. If you lack this confidence, you are not likely to be effective. For example, consider the following request that a nonmedical therapist might make to a physician: "I'm seeing a man who's very tense, almost agitated. We've met four times, and he seems worse now than he was a month ago. Would you be willing to see him for a medication evaluation? I don't think psychotherapy is right for him." This request reflects uncertainty, a lack of confidence in both yourself and the client, and a wish to dilute your relationship with the client when you are most needed. Nonetheless, numerous requests of this type are made daily.

Ideally, in those rare instances where medication may be a necessary adjunct to effective therapy, you should be in a position to make the following type of request, which is not apt to be successful unless you have a working alliance with a physician: "I'm seeing a client who has recurrent, debilitating, and unpredictable panic attacks. They're often accompanied by dizziness. I think he may need Imiprimine to help him regain control. Would you meet with this client, and, if you agree with my evaluation, write a prescription for Imiprimine starting at 25 mg. daily, increasing to 150 mg. daily on the sixth day. I'll continue to see him regularly and keep my eye out for the possible side effects. I'll speak with you again in three or four weeks and let you know how things are going." This request is quite different from the previous one and is the type of request that is most likely to be helpful. It reflects a willingness to continue the counseling relationship with a distressed client. Such a request cannot be made unless you know the relevant parameters (e.g., likelihood of effectiveness, time needed for therapeutic effects to appear, dosage level, side effects) of a wide variety of drugs.

There are two books that are invaluable to the therapist who wishes to be well informed about psychoactive medications. One is the encyclopedic *Physician's Desk Reference*, published annually with a supplement by the Medical Economics Company. This book, often referred to as the *"PDR,"* contains a summary of important information on every available prescription drug. Honigfeld & Howard's 1978 work, *Psychiatric Drugs: A Desk Reference*, second edition, is brief, readable, and indispensable. The authors have a thorough knowledge of psychoactive medications, psychological processes, and how the two interact. Their book contains invaluable information on dosage levels and side effects. Also, it includes many clinical insights and suggestions that will help you identify those clients who might benefit from medication.

Although I will not discuss every psychoactive drug in this chapter, there is one that needs to be discussed in some detail. Although it has proven helpful to a broad range of clients and has been available for a very long while, it is prescribed rarely. Indeed, it seems so powerful and so versatile that, paradoxically, physicians seem reluctant to prescribe it at all; and, nonmedical therapists consulting with physicians seldom mention it. Moreover, unlike other drugs, which often are accompanied by a litany of undesired side effects, this one rarely produces any. And, when it does, the effects tend to be minor (Shapiro & Morris, 1978).

If you have not guessed the name of this drug yet, let me tell you some more about it. Its cost is minimal and has remained stable for years. In an era of cost-effectiveness considerations, when it is not unusual for a hospital to charge a dollar for a cotton ball or an aspirin tablet, this in itself is no small accomplishment. Countless double-blind studies have found this drug to be as effective as its more expensive, more frequently prescribed counterparts, even when the latter are accompanied by life-threatening or permanently debilitating side effects. Admittedly, we do not know the precise site of action of this drug or the complex physiological and psychological mechanisms by which it works. But, since this information remains unknown for virtually all other psychoactive drugs, that uncertainty should not deter us from considering its benefits.

As with most other drugs, it would take a book as long as this one to report in detail the major findings of all the studies in which it has been used and proven effective. However, to indicate the range of this drug's effectiveness, a few such studies will be mentioned. This drug has been found to be at least as effective as the more toxic, more expensive one typically prescribed in the treatment of manic disorders (Chambers & Naylor, 1978), narcotic addiction (Chappel, Jaffe, & Senay, 1974), nonpsychotic depression (Olson, Bank, & Jarvik, 1978), anxiety neurosis (Rickels, Case, Csanalosi, Pereira, Sandler, & Schless, 1978), insomnia (Wang & Stockdale, 1977), schizophrenia (Fredericks & Finkle, 1978; Gross, 1960; Leff & Wing, 1971; Pasamanick, Scarpitti, & Lefton 1967), and acute and chronic pain (Sobel, 1980).

By now you probably have guessed that this medication is the placebo— the empty capsule, the "sugar pill," any inert substance known to be chemicaly irrelevant to the problem at hand.

The placebo's effectiveness reminds us that our knowledge of psychoactive drugs is crude. Trial and error often characterize attempts to identify the "right" dose of the "right" drug for a particular client. If Thorazine does not help, Mellaril may be tried. If that does not "work," perhaps a switch will be made to Haldol, or Loxitane, or Stelazine. With one client, 100 mg. of Librium a day may appear to produce a desired change. Another person, with highly similar symptoms, may be unresponsive to 200 or even 300 mg. a day of Librium; other benzodiazepines may prove equally ineffective. And, once an effective dose of a particular drug is found for a particular individual, troublesome symptoms may reappear nonetheless a few weeks or months later, and the whole process may be set in motion again.

Psychoactive medications are prescribed in *great* disproportion to what we know about them and to their demonstrated effectiveness. Many forces, forces difficult to resist, contribute to this phenomenon. For example, many clients seek and expect immediate and easy relief once they decide to see a counselor or therapist. Some are initially very disappointed and critical when this relief is withheld. All of us have great demands on our time, and it can be tempting to medicate a client rather than initiate psychotherapy. Another factor is the persistent but fading belief that psychological and interpersonal problems are primarily chemical in origin. And, we cannot overlook the effects of the multimillion dollar drug company advertising campaigns that encourage us all to consider psychoactive drugs virtually whenever detectable psychological discomfort exists.

There is no denying that psychoactive drugs can produce dramatic changes in mood. But, when a person swallows a psychoactive medication, there are many processes—in addition to the complex and poorly understood chemical ones—that are set in motion and that contribute to these changes. The person's response to the drug can be influenced by his or her relationship with the person who prescribed it, the confidence these two individuals have in each other, and their hopes and expectations regarding the drug (Cousins, 1979). Other forces can operate as well. For example, a client's family may be encouraged and relieved greatly once a concrete solution—one not available to them previously—is provided. This sort of relief can reduce stress before the prescription is filled. On the other hand, client and family alike can be very disappointed when chemotherapy is resisted and "just" counseling is offered. Or, a drug may fail to produce a desired response because of the discouragement or tension that its use may produce. For example, some may conclude that their therapist thinks they are mentally ill or has abandoned hope in their ability to cope independently.

In short, a wide range of processes can be set in motion when a prescription is written and a drug ingested. These nonchemical processes are referred to as the "placebo effect." Since this effect can dramatically help, hinder, or complicate the therapeutic relationship, it deserves serious attention. The placebo effect can be powerful and can be employed by the effective counselor whether a drug is prescribed or not. You can help a client seek an *internal* solution rather than an *external* one prepared by a pharmacist. You can inject hope without a needle.

I wish to point out yet another reason for using psychoactive drugs only after all else has failed. Even when a drug is taken and is "effective," and even if we could know that it was the chemical itself that produced the desired change, its effectiveness may have had nothing whatsoever to do with the origin of the client's distress. "While drenching with water may help in putting out a blaze, few are the cases in which fire has its origins in a lack of water (Dubos, 1959, p. 86)." Psychoactive drugs may thus distract both client and counselor from the original source of the client's discomfort.

Next, I will discuss three other reasons for avoiding psychoactive medications whenever possible. They interfere with both assessment and therapy; they are accompanied by a variety of side effects; they have not proven to be cost-effective.

DRUGS, ASSESSMENT, AND THERAPY

Once a client is medicated, accurate assessment is not possible. As mentioned above, chemotherapy is apt to produce a number of complex chemical and nonchemical reactions, each of which will influence the counseling relationship. Unless you spend a great deal of time trying to sort out and identify these reactions, you have no way of knowing how that person would be functioning without the prescription. Further, your recommendation of medication may interfere with a client's attempts at self-help. Although a drug may provide some relief, it also may invoke images of dependency, illness, and the need for prolonged, external help. An individual struggling to cope and to change—alone, with family, or with you—may be less likely to do so with the same enthusiasm after the problem and its solution are assessed, even in part, as chemical. Moreover, some will be discouraged by the continued need for a professional to maintain and monitor treatment. This would seem to be a clear example of the assessment process slowing down rather than accelerating development.

Clearly, chemotherapy and effective psychotherapy are quite different; and it is difficult, indeed, to imagine someone doing both with the same client. And, it would seem equally incompatible to recommend to a client that someone else conduct chemotherapy while you conduct psychotherapy. Your recommendation of chemotherapy will interfere with your ability to provide each of the five necessary therapist characteristics described in chapter 1—empathy, composure, readiness to discuss everything, encouragement, and purposefulness. A brief discussion of each of these five qualities will underscore the importance of avoiding advocating chemotherapy until you temporarily have abandoned hope for psychotherapy.

Once a client's mood is altered chemically, it becomes impossible to *empathize* with the feelings and thoughts that led that person to you initially and that would be present if the medication was not being taken. The client, too, is apt to lose touch with the troublesome feeling. Valium, for example, may "take the edge off" someone's tension, but what then? It would seem that the three options available are discussion of a feeling that is now muted or nonexistent, continuation of Valium in lieu of counseling, or decreasing the dosage of Valium with the hope that it will be discontinued altogether. And, if this third option is tried, why prescribe it in the first place? Whenever possible, even if someone's tension, for example, seems unbearable, explore fully the limits of an empathic relationship, even if this requires daily visits for a while. Help the client identify and alleviate the internal or environmental sources of tension.

Another trait a helper must offer a client is *composure*. Yet, medications often are introduced into the therapeutic relationship when the therapist has lost that composure (DiGiacomo & Cornfield, 1979; Stein, 1975). Without question, psychotherapy can be very difficult work for client and counselor alike. It is an understatement to say that it can be very difficult to remain calm and composed in the face of intense anger, tension, or despondency. A chemical to lift the spirits of a despondent client can provide relief to the therapist as well as the client who swallows it.

But, although such a step may provide short-term relief, it may not be helpful. Some clients will draw strength and optimism from your composure during difficult moments. Conversely, you may unintentionally confirm a client's worst fears if you recommend medication during a difficult period. This recommendation can stimulate a person to conclude that his or her feelings frighten you and that you will not discuss them unless they are diluted.

Avoid calling upon medication to make *your* day more manageable. Make a special effort to work with only a limited number of acutely distressed people at any one time. For example, do not work with more than one—or at the most, two—acutely "suicidal" individuals at any one time. If a second or third one comes along, for your sake and for theirs, rather than medicate, first refer them effectively to a competent colleague who is not overburdened with such clients.

Regarding *readiness to discuss everything*, a client is likely to conclude that you do not wish to discuss a certain mood or thought when, after it is mentioned, you indicate that medication may be needed. Tofranil, for example, may dilute feelings of despondency, but it also is likely to dilute the need to discuss those feelings. And, as above, if *you* find it difficult to discuss a certain topic, make an appropriate referral rather than indirectly discourage a willing client from examining it.

When a client requests medication because of a wish to avoid a certain feeling or thought, you should respond to that request as you would any other. Namely, discuss it. Try to help the client identify the wishes and feelings that may underlie the request rather than merely grant or deny it. For some reason, certain therapists who *would* examine possibly simple requests for, say, more or less frequent visits, longer or shorter visits, or permission to pay a bill late, do not examine a request for medication in the same way. Rather, they consider the request as a strong indication that medication is, in fact, needed; and they are apt to grant the request shortly thereafter. This is a curious, significant example of a therapist's *un*willingness to discuss everything.

Another necessary therapist characteristic is *encouragement*. Some clients may find it encouraging to be handed a prescription that they hope represents a concrete solution to their troubles. But, would they be encouraged if they knew about all of the possible side effects, the possibility of addiction, or that they may be back where they started once the medication is discontinued? Other clients are apt to be discouraged when they are told, in so many words, "Your problem requires a type of solution which you cannot provide for yourself. In fact, psychotherapy won't be enough, either."

A number of clients have told me that they were encouraged when I indicated to them that, despite the intensity of their problems, I felt that their internal resources and the potential of our relationship was such that medication was not necessary. In fact, a number of people have disclosed to me that they inquired about medication hoping that I would advise against it. Some individuals may use your response to such an inquiry as a measure of the confidence you have in their ability to cope.

Last but not least, the use of psychoactive medications is not consistent with the *purposefulness* characteristic of effective therapists. For, intimately associated with this purposefulness is an eye toward short-term counseling, usually lasting no longer than ten sessions. As pointed out in chapter 1, regardless of a counselor's orientation, clients resist long-term therapeutic relationships. And, although "long-term" at the turn of the century could mean six or seven years, it now typically means six or seven months. Chemotherapy is highly incompatible with a short-term approach. It is not at all uncommon, for example, for it to take several months merely to find the desired dosage level of the most effective drug for any one client. It can take "a minimum trial period of 3-4 weeks (Honigfeld & Howard, 1978)" to determine if an antidepressant is proving effective, and, sometimes, three or four different antidepressants must be tried before the most effective one is found. Moreover, different dosage levels may need to be explored with each drug; and it is often recommended that, when switching from one drug to another, a seven to ten day "wash out" period be observed during which no medication is administered. Even once this lengthy process is complete, many continued visits are necessary to, hopefully, gradually decrease the dosage level and to monitor for side effects, many of which appear for the first time several months after chemotherapy was initiated.

Before presenting experimental support for the notion that chemotherapy is inconsistent with assessment and psychotherapy, I wish to say a word about the special case in which a client requests psychotherapy from you while simultaneously receiving chemotherapy from someone else. As implied above, I believe that it is extremely difficult—if not impossible—to conduct psychotherapy and chemotherapy at the same time with the same person. This is true regardless of whether you prescribe the medication or request a colleague to do so. However, it is possible to engage in psychotherapy with a client who is taking psychoactive drugs prescribed by another individual, provided that you have not encouraged the chemotherapy in any way whatsoever.

Indeed, so many individuals are "on" antianxiety drugs and antidepressants that it is a good idea, during assessment, to ask each client what medications, if any, they have taken within the last six weeks or so. If you are to do effective work with those individuals who are taking psychoactive drugs, you will need to explore with them their attitudes toward the medication and toward the individual who prescribed it. A client who begins work with you after chemotherapy has been initiated may be dissatisfied with that approach and may be on the verge of discontinuing it. On the other hand, if a client begins drug therapy with someone else during psychotherapy with you, this can reflect dissatisfaction with you. In either case, the client cannot help but benefit from the opportunity to explore his attitudes, feelings, and hopes for the two differing approaches. Such a discussion is apt to strengthen both your relationship with the client and the client's belief that the medication is not needed.

Next, I wish to discuss some experimental evidence for the notion that psychoactive medications interfere with assessment and counseling. Since psychiatrists often line up on one side of this issue and nonphysicians on the other, I will begin this brief review with a study conducted by three physicians. As emphasized in chapter 1, in order to best serve those who come to us for help, each of us must avoid knee–jerk opinions thought to be dictated by our particular profession. Carpenter, McGlashan, and Strauss (1977), three physicians, conducted a long-term study of 122 "acute schizophrenics." Importantly, this diagnostic group is thought by many to have benefited most from the era of modern psychopharmacology. In the study, 49 individuals were treated at the National Institute of Health with a sharply limited use of psychoactive medications. For these 49 people, psychosocial treatment was emphasized. Their progress was compared to that of 73 similarly diagnosed individuals treated in the "usual" manner, namely, with primary reliance on phenothiazines.

After two years, using several different outcome measures, a small but statistically significant superiority was found in the former, limited medication, group. Moreover, within this group, there was no difference whatsoever between the 22 who received minimal medication over the two years and the 27 who received none. The authors concluded, "The treatment of schizophrenia has become so extensively drug oriented that a significant impediment has arisen to the exploration of alternative therapeutic approaches. . . . No other disorder in the history of psychiatry has had a richer panoply of global claims to its cause and cure [pp. 14, 15]." The authors also noted that premature drug administration can make accurate assessment impossible.

Carpenter et al. also present and discuss several deficiencies in the literature that supports phenothiazine use. For example, the authors note a lack of long-range follow-up studies and common use of inappropriate outcome measures. To be sure, large doses of, say, Thorazine may accelerate discharge. But, in over half the cases, discharge will be followed by relapse and readmission in less than one year. Moreover, Carpenter et al. concluded that phenothiazine treatment may *increase* the relapse rate and that "relapse during drug administration is greater in severity than when no drugs are given [p. 18]."

We should all strive for the thoroughness, objectivity, and ethical sensitivity of these three authors whenever we engage in psychotherapy or conduct or review research. They "found it possible to use a research strategy for investigating drug-free schizophrenic patients, while maintaining a responsible therapeutic approach to those patients within the framework of a medical model [p. 20]."

Medication is advocated frequently for older clients although here, too, it has been found to interfere with both assessment and counseling. Covert, Rodrigues, and Solomon (1977), for example, describe some dangers of using psychotropic medications with elderly clients. To support their opinions, they cite a number of actual cases in which psychoactive drugs either exacerbated or totally masked physical or psychological problems and thus denied the clients an adequate assessment.

Another type of client for whom medication is commonly prescribed is the older person who seeks a counselor following the death of a spouse. Although this approach often appears to be effective and efficient, Mayer (1975) has concluded that drug-induced inhibition of grief prevents completion of the adaptive mourning process and, in the long run, creates more difficulties than it solves. Chemical treatment of the grieving process also can complicate matters with the young. Dopson (1979) describes the case of a 15-year-old who developed factitious lymphedema in her right hand and arm on the first anniversary of the death of her grandmother who died because of the failure of the pacemaker implanted in her right arm. Prescription of medication to decrease the swelling complicated and prolonged the young woman's treatment. Even a medication prescribed for a "physical" problem can interfere with the counselor's assessment and treatment.

Finally, many fail to consider the effect that chemotherapy may have on a client's family. Mayo, O'Connell, and O'Brian (1979) studied the families of twelve individuals who were *successfully* treated with lithium for "bipolar manic–depressive illness." The authors found an unexpected "side effect," namely, family members of the clients continued to need psychotherapeutic assistance but lost contact with the therapist because the clients' symptoms had been eliminated. In other words, we may lose contact with a number of individuals who need our help if we mask or diminish symptoms prematurely.

I draw two conclusions from these five studies. First, whenever possible, avoid the use of psychoactive drugs. Even when the case for using these drugs seems the strongest (e.g., in acute schizophrenia, manic-depressive disorders, and with the depressed elderly), they have been shown to prolong treatment and interfere with assessment, and they have failed to demonstrate effectiveness with any consistency. Second, there is a strong need for more interaction between medical and nonmedical workers. It is tragic indeed when a problem that is primarily physical, such as a brain tumor, is treated as a psychological problem because of its symptoms. It can be equally tragic when a problem that is primarily psychological, such as the swelling in the Dopson study, is treated primarily as medical. Close collaboration between physician and nonphysician is needed for the proper care of many individuals.

For a myriad of troubles, the temptation to medicate is great. Psychoactive medications may provide a prompt reduction in symptoms and consequently lead a client to lose interest in counseling. Many workers consider this a blessing, since demands on our time are great and promise to increase in the years ahead. However, many have concluded that these drugs, in the long run, create at least as many problems as they solve. Their benefits may be illusory. Moreover, your recommendation of their use would seem to render it impossible for you to then provide a client with the therapist characteristics described in chapter 1.

SIDE EFFECTS AND DESIRED EFFECTS

There is yet another reason to refrain from prematurely involving a client with medication. Many changes may occur when an individual takes a drug such as Valium, Thorazine, or Ritalin. The change that is hoped for often is referred to as the desired effect; the other, undesired, changes are referred to as side effects. Even when the desired effect is achieved, it may be equaled or overshadowed by the damage done or new problems created by these, so-called "side" effects. Often, as information regarding a particular drug accumulates, new side effects are discovered. Only after Valium had been in use for many years, for example, was it discovered that it has the potential to be addictive after long-term use. Similarly, only recently have we recognized the frequency of occurrence of tardive dyskinesia, "usually consisting of uncontrolled, arrhythmic movements particularly of the nose, cheeks, tongue, or throat and sometimes involving shaking of the feet or hands [Honigfeld & Howard, 1979, p. 25]." This disorder is irreversible in many cases and can appear suddenly after one dose of a phenothiazine. In other cases, it takes many years to appear, and, in still other cases, it does not appear until phenothiazine treatment is discontinued. One cannot help but wonder if similar—or even more severe—side effects will be documented after data are collected on the long-term use of the newer drugs.

Each psychoactive medication is accompanied by numerous, less dramatic, side effects. I think many clients taking these medications would be horrified if they knew of them. Admittedly, the *PDR* lists every known side effect for each drug, even those that occur quite infrequently. Agranulocytosis, for example, is a sharp drop in white blood cell count associated with high fever and a serious risk of death due to a lessened resistance to infection. "The incidence of this side effect among patients on antipsychotic drug therapy is about 1 in 1000 [Honigfeld & Howard, 1979, p. 91]." These odds are highly favorable, but they do not matter much if you are the "1." Indeed, the very first person I knew who took Thorazine, the most widely-used antipsychotic medication, developed agranulocytosis and was dead two days later.

Has the usefulness of these drugs been demonstrated to the point that such risks are justified? Although the more severe side effects occur rarely, how many times do they occur each day, when one considers, for example, the many thousands of people taking Thorazine. Even when the desired effect is obtained, could it have been obtained in a *safer* way, such as psychotherapy, a lower dose of the drug, or no dose at all? How many people will spend the rest of their lives taking increasingly high doses of phenothiazines to inhibit the appearance of tardive dyskinesia? How many will be going to the newly-appearing tardive dyskinesia clinics—the latest memorial to the saying, "the medicine is worse than the malady"? Barbiturates are used rarely now, but how many people died unnecessarily before it was discovered that, over time, the effective dose gradually increases and becomes close to the lethal dose, or that "a former user will be unable to tolerate barbiturates in the same high doses to which he was accustomed before drug discontinuation [Honigfeld & Howard, 1979, p. 45]"? How many people have used barbiturates or some other psychoactive medication to commit suicide who would be alive today had the drug not been available to them? To be sure, some people are so desperate and ingenious that they would find a method of self-destruction regardless of how many devices are removed. But, there are others who actively consider suicide by one method only and for them the suicide risk is reduced greatly once that one method is removed.

Even if the prescription of psychoactive drugs did *not* interfere with assessment and therapy, it would seem, because of their side effects, that they should be prescribed with considerably more restraint than they are now. Moreover, every month, a broad array of journals presents us with reports of newly discovered side effects, which account in part for the need for an annual revision of the *PDR* accompanied by semiannual supplements. Recent examples of such reports are the findings of Chouinard and Jones (1980) that, in some cases, antipsychotic agents can induce psychosis; and those of Mitchell and Gillum (1980), who present a case history of a person who developed cardiac arrhythmia as a consequence of treatment of anorexia nervosa with tricyclics.

Moreover, as implied in the previous discussion of barbiturates, some people will abuse these drugs. In one study of 55 consecutively hospitalized individuals who abused sedatives or hypnotics, Bergman, Borg, and Holm

(1980) found significantly more intellectual and neurological impairment in this group than in a matched control group. Bergman et al. concluded that sedative or hypnotic abuse can produce cerebral disorder. As mentioned above in the discussion of tardive dyskinesia, serious problems sometimes do not appear until a drug is discontinued. For example, Santos and McCurdy (1980) describe a 42-year-old man whose delirium apparently was precipitated by abrupt withdrawal from tricyclics. Still another problem is that some people take the medication originally prescribed for someone else. Cavenar and Harris (1980) report a "folie á deux" dystonic reaction in which a man took his wife's haloperidol, developed dystonia, and rushed himself to a clinic. The wife appeared five minutes later at the clinic with identical symptoms. In summary, these drugs, which are risky enough even when taken "correctly," can and will be abused in a variety of ways—often with devastating results.

Moreover, when two drugs are taken by the same individual, new, or greatly intensified, side effects may appear. We know a good deal more about the effects of individual psychoactive drugs than we do about the various ways in which these drugs potentiate each other's side effects or produce new effects when taken together. Although "polypharmacy" usually is not recommended (Honigfeld & Howard, 1979), it is not uncommon for an individual to be taking two, or even three, psychoactive drugs simultaneously. Psychoactive drugs also can interact in harmful ways with other prescription drugs. For example, Blumenthal and Davie (1980) examined 100 psychiatric outpatients, age 60 and older, and found that 40 percent of them complained of dizziness and falling. Drug treatment— especially the combination of tricyclics with hypotension-inducing drugs —was the most significant factor accounting for the dizziness and falling.

In addition to the more dramatic side effects mentioned here, psychoactive drugs frequently produce a number of "minor" but nagging side effects such as dry mouth, sweating, nausea, constipation, and a "zombie-like" appearance associated with the phenothiazines. Increasingly, people are beginning to ask: "Are these drugs worth it?" "Do the benefits of these drugs outweigh—or even equal—their dangers?" Of course, questions such as these must be answered separately for each drug and for each drug class. I will not attempt such a comprehensive review here. But I will summarize below what we know about the phenothiazines, the drug class with the broadest base of professional support.

As it turns out, it is much easier to demonstrate that psychoactive drugs, phenothiazines included, produce *side* effects than it is to demonstrate that they produce *desired* effects. For example, Hollon and Beck (1978) reviewed more than 100 studies in which the effectiveness of psychotherapy was compared to that of chemotherapy. Although some of the studies they reviewed were methodologically sound, they concluded, "by and large, however, the bulk of the studies contain a variety of methodological flaws and restrictions on generality that undermine confidence in conclusions drawn [p. 485]." Their review included many studies of the phenothiazine Thorazine, the most widely used antipsychotic medication. The authors concluded that the chemotherapy literature is in its "infancy." Unless the superiority of chemotherapy is demonstrated with some certainty, it would seem wiser to recommend that a client exhaust the possibilities of psychotherapy first, since psychotherapy only rarely produces side effects.

Many individuals believe that the introduction of the phenothiazines in the mid-1950s was the most significant development in the care of mentally troubled people in this century. These individuals cite as evidence for their point of view the fact that, shortly after these drugs were introduced on a large scale, the number of individuals hospitalized in mental institutions decreased dramatically. However, we should not forget that correlation does not imply causation. The early and mid-1950s were also characterized by a dramatic upsurge in the community mental health movement, a significant increase in the number of individuals entering and graduating from graduate programs in a variety of helping professions, and a growing disenchantment with medical model, accompanied by a commitment to try alternative treatment methods. The role that these and other factors played in the decline in mental hospital census in the 1950s may never be known. Interestingly, Bockoven and Solomon (1975) reviewed two, five-year-followup studies of individuals diagnosed "schizophrenic." One study was done during 1947–1952, before the introduction of phenothiazines; the other was done during 1967–1972, after the introduction. Outcome results in the two studies were equivalent. Over a five-year period, individuals taking phenothiazines did no better than similarly diagnosed individuals before the use of antipsychotic medications.

Research support for phenothiazine use continues to be equivocal. Lonowski, Seterling, and Kennedy (1978), for example, studied 48 hospitalized "chronic schizophrenics," 25 of whom had their medication dosage gradually decreased and 23 of whom had no dosage alteration. After 15 weeks, 74 percent of the drug-decreased and 80 percent of the drug-maintained individuals had decompensated. The authors concluded that maintenance doses of antipsychotic drugs for chronic patients can be eliminated at minimal risk. A similar conclusion was reached by Nair (1977), who studied "chronic schizophrenics" in the community. Indeed, Nair also concluded that low doses of antipsychotic medication may interfere with the reintegration of recently discharged individuals into the community. A study of 820 "chronic schizophrenics" in Greece echoes these results (Manos, Taratsidis, Pappas, & Routsonis, 1977). In this study, medication had no effect on whether or not people were rehospitalized after discharge. Also, medication did not affect the time interval between discharge and rehospitalization. The authors report an increased adaptability of, and social tolerance for, those individuals who discontinued medication altogether. Finally, Gardos and Cole (1976) concluded from their research that about half of all medicated "chronic schizophrenic" outpatients would do as well without the medication.

This consideration of side effects and desired effects leads to three conclusions. First, we need to know much more about psychoactive drugs than we do now (Fauman, 1980; Gay, 1978). Clear-cut evidence of their effectiveness simply does not exist. Second, until we *do* know more about these medications, we should use them with more caution (Greer & Davis, 1977; Loney, 1980). Unless use of a drug clearly *is* indicated, we should not ask a client to endure its side effects. Third, except in those rare instances when chemotherapy clearly *is* indicated, counseling should be initiated instead. Almost never should you attempt to do both with the same client simultaneously. Even though, like chemotherapy, counseling is not always effective, it rarely produces undesired side effects.

COST-EFFECTIVENESS

At this point, you may be saying, "Well, even if these drugs aren't *better* than psychotherapy, perhaps they're worth the risks because they're just as good but less expensive. A pill may cost a dime, or fifty cents, and psychotherapy can cost seventy-five dollars an hour!" As it turns out, however, the little evidence there is regarding comparable cost-effectiveness of the two approaches indicates that psychotherapy is the more cost-effective.

As above, the following discussion of cost-effectiveness will emphasize treatment of "schizophrenia," the disorder thought by many to be the least responsive to psychotherapy. Even here, however, psychotherapy has been found to be the more cost-effective. That is, it has been shown to be more economical than chemotherapy in both tangible and clinical benefits produced by the money spent. During the 1970s, Karon and Vanden Bos (1972, 1975a, 1975b) conducted a number of ground-breaking studies comparing the cost-effectiveness of psychotherapy vs. chemotherapy. They concluded that:

> Psychotherapy, when compared to medication, produces greater decrease in thought disorder, shortened hospitalization, "better" and more human recovery/functioning, and less long-term hospitalization. . . . Effective psychotherapy saves money . . . particularly in the *long run*. . . . Adjunctive use of medication with psychotherapy makes behavioral control and early initial discharge from the hospital easier, but slows psychotherapeutic improvement in the basic underlying thought disorder and consequently tends to diminish the long term effectiveness of psychotherapy [1975b, pp. 1, 4].

Karon and Vanden Bos believe that medications provoke a revolving-door policy in which medicated clients are discharged quickly from the hospital but readmitted more often than not. On the other hand, they found that unmedicated clients spent about half as much time in institutions. Since hospital and drug costs have escalated much more rapidly than psychotherapy costs in recent years, Karon and Vanden Bos' conclusions would seem more valid now than they were in the early and mid-1970s.

In 1979, Deikman and Whitaker reached similar conclusions. Over a one-year period, they converted a psychiatric ward with a primary reliance on drugs to a ward using an intensive psychological approach, with drugs virtually abolished. They found the latter, psychotherapy-oriented, approach "superior in long-term cost/benefit effectiveness to the prevalent 'revolving door' programs which emphasize drugs and 'dischargeability.' . . . Much more is possible in the psychological treatment of severely disturbed patients than is usually believed [pp. 204, 212]."

Some studies have failed to demonstrate the comparable cost-effectiveness of psychotherapy (e.g., May, 1968; Tuma & May, 1974). However, in a thorough, objective review of such studies, Karon and Vanden Bos (1975a) found a substantial number of methodological shortcomings. For example, "In every study where psychotherapy has not been helpful, quality control of *relevant* training, experience, and motivation has not been maintained [p. 148]." Some of the other weaknesses they cite in these studies:

> were . . . gross discontinuity (termination) of the psychotherapy at discharge from the hospital, inconsistent timing of evaluations, contaminated criteria of outcome, and idiosyncratic data analyses (including, among other things, procedures which eliminated the sickest patients from consideration) [p. 143].

With increasing frequency, studies are appearing which find psychotherapy, relaxation training, or treatment by paraprofessionals more cost-effective than chemotherapy. For example, Kazdin (1978) presents a comprehensive literature review supporting the conclusion that reinforcement techniques— which can be administered by paraprofessionals—are more cost-effective than either Ritalin or Thorazine in controlling hyperactive or aggressive behavior in children. Allyon, Layman, and Kandel (1975) found the cost-effectiveness of reinforcement techniques equal to that of Ritalin in suppressing hyperactive behavior of children in a classroom situation. McLean and Hakstian (1979), in a study of 178 depressed clients, found no difference in cost-effectiveness between chemotherapy and relaxation training.

Again, it cannot be emphasized too strongly that, unless chemotherapy has demonstrated superiority over an alternative mode of treatment (e.g., counseling, relaxation training, reinforcement programs), *the alternative should be tried first*. This is true for three reasons. First, the alternative will not be accompanied by side effects. Second, the alternative is likely to be less expensive. Third, the alternative will be more likely to furnish the hope that the client can deal with the problem at hand without long-term, chemical care and attention.

CONCLUSIONS

I wish to conclude with a few more comments about placebos and the placebo effect. As pointed out in the early pages of this chapter, even when a drug *seems* to be effective, factors other than the chemical in the capsule can, in fact, be the cause of the change. Hopes, expectations, and the client's personality can play a very significant role in determining the response to what is ingested (Levine & Sice, 1976). For example, Mintz (1977) reports the case of a 38-year-old woman accustomed to taking large doses of Ritalin, who, unknowingly, was switched over to a placebo instead. In one year, she took about 1,000 placebos and never knew the difference.

The enthusiasm of the person prescribing the medication is also very important. Indeed, after a review of more than 250 studies, Shapiro and Morris (1978) concluded that the success of chemotherapy for psychological disorders depends more on the enthusiasm of the doctor prescribing it than on any other factor. Evans and di Scipio (1980) reached similar conclusions regarding the importance of "nonpharmacologic factors" in a study of 47 adolescents medicated at a psychiatric center. Cummings (1979) believes that personality factors are more important than chemical ones even when powerful "addictive" drugs are involved. He writes, "The concept of addiction as a disease is useless because it implies that one is helpless and cannot do anything about it. . . . So I say to my clients, 'Do not ask me what is addictive and what is not, if you are an addictive personality, you can even get addicted to water [p. 1121]."

The following statement of Jourard (1968) highlights the important, powerful, nonpharmacologic factors that can operate when a drug is prescribed:

> Neurotics complain about the price one must pay for safety. They withdraw from authenticity to be safe; but being withdrawn, they experience loneliness, boredom, or the dread of being found out. When a neurotic sufferer goes to a therapist to get help with his anxiety and loneliness, he calls them symptoms. The therapist says, in effect, "You don't like these symptoms. They seem to be connected with your withdrawal. You want to get rid of those symptoms. Then, stop withdrawing." The fellow says, "No, can't you give me some tranquilizers, so I can stay withdrawn and be anesthetized? I'll be glad to pay this

additional price of being numb." Unfortunately too many therapists will give them a tranquilizer. That's one good thing about being a psychologist. You dare not use drugs. This puts you on your mettle. I have one instance where I "malpracticed medicine." I prescribed a "drug," Quik cocoa. A patient said he couldn't sleep. He had been getting sleeping pills. I thought I understood what was going on. I said, "I know how to get to sleep." I said it with great certainty, because I have great faith in it. "At bedtime, you get some milk and put it in a saucepan. You boil it over a very slow flame. (The slower the better.) You keep testing it with your finger until you can't stand it, short of boiling. Then, you put in two tablespoons of instant cocoa, Nestlé's Quik. Oh, any kind will do." I don't want to specialize in any one brand. "Then once you have mixed it up in a cup, you get vanilla wafers, and I specify any kind of vanilla wafers. You dip them in and eat them, and sip the hot cocoa. If you haven't got vanilla wafers, then get white or wheat toast, lightly toasted with butter melted in it and then spread apple jelly on it. (Grape jelly is too strong.) You take it and you will fall asleep practically before you finish it." I have never had a complaint from this. This has weaned a lot of people from sleeping pills and tranquilizers. I feel vaguely guilty about this because it is like a prescription. That's too much like practicing medicine [p. 83].*

Psychoactive drugs have been shown to be more toxic and more expensive than other forms of help. They have rarely proven to be more effective than even the placebo. This is true even for those disorders thought to be *most* responsive to chemotherapy and *least* responsive to psychotherapy (e.g., schizophrenia, hyperactivity in children). Try to keep this in mind the next time you consider having a client medicated. And, the next time a client inquires about medication, try to help the person identify the feelings that lie beneath the request. Is the person feeling overwhelmed? Is the person giving up hope in you, in the therapeutic relationship, or in him- or herself? Attempts to answer such questions are an essential part of effective counseling. If you feel medication must be offered, do so for as brief a time as possible and only if you believe the medication will be associated with a sudden, noticeable change in the client that will be encouraging and will set the stage for therapy. Otherwise, attempts to medicate are likely to lead the client down a dark, dead-end road.

Chapter 6
Crossroads

A word in season spoken
May calm the troubled breast.
            —Charles Jefferys,
            A Word in Season

As implied in each of the previous chapters, you will need to choose your words with great care if you are to be an effective therapist. Psychotherapy is, for the most part, a verbal endeavor, and most clients usually will be listening very carefully to what you have to say. More often than not, however, you will have an opportunity to clarify an occasional confusing or unhelpful remark. Typically, the fate of the counseling relationship will not hinge on any one of your comments. However, certain crucial moments will arise which *will* require a personal, effective response from you at that time. When these occur, you will need to choose your words not with great care but with *very* great care. Now and then, there will be no second chance.

Some of these moments will be especially important because of the intensity of the client's distress at the time. Other, less dramatic moments can be equally important because they are one-of-a-kind events from which a client is apt to draw broad generalizations. Below, I will discuss a number of these crucial moments and what I have said when they have occurred. You may wish to treat these situations as I have, but that is not necessary. But it is necessary that you realize that, now and then, there will be turning points which you will need to recognize and respond to effectively. Moreover, I hope this presenation will encourage you to think of additional crucial moments that are not identified here. I will discuss these under three broad headings: The Telephone, The Suicidal Client, and When You Feel Bewildered.

75

THE TELEPHONE

Up to this point, I have described counseling as a face-to-face venture that occurs in an office. But, not all clients will allow you to keep it that simple. Inevitably, some will want to speak with you on the telephone. They may call when you are at home or at the office. They may call to make a first appointment, to reschedule an appointment, or to tell you that they have decided life is not worth living. Such telephone calls are apt to be considerably important, regardless of their content. For, they often reflect the ambivalence of clients who are not sure enough of you (or themselves) to come to your office, but who do care enough to call. Your effectiveness on the telephone will, in many instances, determine whether or not psychotherapy begins or continues.

It is important, therefore, that you be very "reachable" by telephone. If you are difficult to get through to at home, too busy at the office to receive calls, or if it takes you several days to return a call, you will be perceived as remote and disinterested. This will happen even if you are *not* that way and even if those people would get a more accurate picture of you from one or several face-to-face encounters. Many people draw hasty conclusions and will not give a second chance to the provider of *any* service who seems remote, abrupt, or disinterested. This comment would seem especially true for an anxious or ambivalent client appraising a counselor via the telephone. Moreover, a person who is considering making an initial appointment with you may decide not to once he or she hears that you are "impossible to get through to" on the telephone, and that, in essence, you will speak with them only "when the meter is running." On the other hand, your availability may help strengthen fragile relationships and may ease the way for those who are considering seeing you for the first time.

There is no way to predict who will want to phone you, when, and for what reason. Consequently, try to let as many people as possible know that you are more than willing to be phoned at any time at the office or at home. Very few people will abuse your willingness to speak with them on the telephone. Many professionals discourage telephone calls from consumers, and people may assume that this is true of you, also, unless you make it a point to notify them otherwise. In any printed advertising or announcements you provide (e.g., the yellow pages, brochures, or information sheets supplied at your office), include a sentence or phrase indicating how you, personally, can be reached by telephone. Also, I think it is important to include both your home and office telephone numbers in such announcements. These steps will make it quite a bit easier for the tentative, ambivalent client, or for the person who is not yet a client, to speak with you briefly and safely.

Sadly, many professionals go to great lengths to avoid any telephone work with clients. Some routinely bill clients for all time spent on the telephone. Others do not list their home telephone number in the telephone book or list it in an obscure manner, making it next to impossible for a client to reach them "after hours."

With certain clients, your availability and sensitivity on the telephone will make the difference between success and failure. Also, some clients will precede the first visit with a reconnaissance phone call, designed both to evaluate you and to obtain information. For example, I have been asked by strangers on the telephone: "Dr. Brenner, I think I'm impotent. My last three attempts at sex have been a disaster. Can you help me?" "Dr. Brenner, can I make an appointment with you without leaving my name?" "Dr. Brenner, what is your fee?" If you are not readily available to people who wish to ask such questions, or if you try to have a secretary or answering machine routinely intercept such calls, you may never get to meet certain people who are within a whisker of making their first appointment. Similarly, I suspect that numerous abrupt and puzzling terminations have been preceded by unreturned or unsatisfactory telephone calls.

As mentioned above, most clients will phone only when it is quite necessary. Once, a client phoned me at the office, and, in a calm voice, told the secretary that she wanted to speak with me. The secretary said, "Dr. Brenner is in a meeting now that will be over in about fifteen minutes. May he return your call then, or would you like to speak with him now?" The woman replied, "Now." The secretary then asked her to hang on for a moment and described the conversation to me. I then ended the appointment with the client in my office, and we scheduled another one. (With a different client, or if the meeting had just begun, I might have asked the client to wait in the reception area until the telephone conversation was over and then resumed the session.) I then said "Hello" to the caller. As soon as she heard my voice, she began sobbing deeply and speaking incoherently. She managed to explain to me that she was just about to go for a ride with her father, who appeared to be sleeping or resting on the steering wheel as she was walking toward the car. But, when she got inside the car and tried to wake him, she discovered he was dead. We spoke for about thirty minutes, and she regained her composure. We decided to meet the next day. In that session, and in the ones to follow, it became quite clear that it was *very* important to her that I was "there" when she felt she most needed me, for she had been very hurt in the past by people who had abandoned or ignored her in moments of need. Our phone conversation helped her believe that I (and, by implication, others) would not treat her in this manner. I have no doubt that this call represented an important crossroads in our relationship and in her broader life as well.

This incident illustrates four important points. First, this woman felt I was someone she could turn to and telephone in an emergency. Clients are not apt to phone you in an emergency or urgent situation unless you tell them, sincerely, that they can. If you make it difficult for clients to speak with you on the telephone, you may forfeit your best opportunity to help. Second, follow each client's lead regarding when the two of you will speak on the telephone. Typically, you will be called only now and then, and with good reason. And, even when a client "abuses" the opportunity and phones excessively, the existence and content of the calls is apt to be a source of necessary grist for the therapeutic mill. In short, trust the client's judgment. Third, it is necessary that you provide guidelines to any person (e.g., family members, a colleague, a secretary) who might answer a client's telephone call. Your wishes will not matter much if someone responds to a request to speak with you with, "I'm sorry, Dr. Brenner is busy now and cannot be interrupted." Or, for example, if you are willing to speak with anonymous callers, make sure that people who receive your calls avoid an automatic, "Who's calling, please?" Any insensitivity, rudeness, or indifference of telephone workers inevitably will limit *your* effectiveness as a counselor.

A word should be said about the client in the above example whose session was ended precipitously. Although this has happened to only a handful of clients, each has found it to be beneficial for one reason or another. For example, some have told me that it made them feel good to help someone indirectly by stepping aside so that I might speak with a person who seemed to need me more at that moment. Others have indicated that it was comforting to learn, firsthand, that I would make every effort to respond to *them* promptly if they ever wanted to speak with me in a hurry. Contrary to what might be expected, this type of intrusion never has interfered with—and occasionally has accelerated—therapeutic progress of the person whose session was interrupted.

Willing and creative use of the telephone can enhance substantially your effectiveness as a counselor. But, we all have our limits, and I have found that I am not at my best—or even close to it—when I am awakened by telephone in the dark of night by a client who wants to discuss a very important matter with me while I am half asleep. At first, I tried to conceal, ignore, or instantaneously overcome my sleepiness. Now, I am very candid with late-night callers, saying something like:

> It's OK that you phoned. I can tell from the sound of your voice that you are quite upset. But, as you can probably tell, I just woke up, and I doubt that I can be of much help to you right now. Can you phone back—or can I phone you—in about fifteen minutes or so. I'll be fully awake then. Or, even better, can you come into the office at 8:30 tomorrow morning? I think I'll be more able to help you if we can see each other while we're talking and if we know we can't be overheard.

Here, I have found that my "effectiveness" has grown out of my recognition of the importance of being honest about my limitations. Indeed, immediately after such a comment, some clients have told me that they were very tired (or intoxicated), and that they welcomed the opportunity to talk the following morning. It took many years before I felt comfortable telling a client in acute distress that I needed some time before I could be of much help. So far, I have found that even the most acutely disturbed client has responded well to my somewhat surprising display of honesty. Most have chosen to come in the next morning. Some have phoned back, or had me phone them later. All of these callers seem to have benefited both from my recognition of the importance of the moment to them and from my authentic, personal comment. Although it is not at all necessary that you respond as I do in this situation, it is very important that you recognize the importance of this turning point and that you reply in a helpful way.

Also, as implied in the above example, I keep about thirty minutes of time unscheduled, even on the busiest of days, so that I easily can accommodate a person who wants to talk with me "right away" or "as soon as possible" without significant inconvenience. Moreover, it will be helpful to many clients to know that there is a time each day that you are in your office, alone. People who are temporarily highly fragile or insecure, or who are closely involved with a very unpredictable friend or family member, for example, will be reassured to know that there is a particular time each day when they may phone you—or even see you—without major inconvenience to anyone. If clients sense that an unscheduled discussion with you is apt to cause significant inconvenience to you, a secretary, or other clients, they will tend to stay away for that reason. Many counselors, unwittingly perhaps, limit their effectiveness by failing to include, routinely, a certain amount of flexibility in their daily schedule.

THE SUICIDAL CLIENT

If clients tend to feel comfortable being candid with you, there is little doubt that, over the years, a number of them will tell you that they are thinking either of hurting themselves in some way or of taking their own life. Indeed, some people may come to you to discuss these thoughts, regardless of whether or not you feel prepared to become involved in that type of relationship. If you have been recommended by a friend, for example, or if a client has found you to be helpful in your early sessions together, these thoughts or feelings are apt to be shared with you. Some clients will not consider your profession, training, or previous experience as relevant. And, although a referral to someone "more qualified" may work out well, the person who has decided to confide in you may feel rejected and may not follow through. If the person has decided that you are the one and only person to be trusted, it is very doubtful that such a referral would be successful.

My first suggestion to you is that *whenever* a person tells you that he or she is contemplating suicide, take it seriously. I always have been very puzzled by those professionals who try to discount some suicidal ideation as "just a manipulation" or an attempt to "get attention." I think, similarly, that you can find much better ways to utilize your assessment skills than to try to distinguish between suicide "gestures" and "attempts." This is an unreliable—perhaps false—dichotomy, like others discussed in chapter 3. Once a person is dead or permanently injured, does it matter if they "really" wanted to hurt themselves or if they were "just trying to get attention"? At the crucial moment when a client tells you that he or she is considering suicide, *first* do everything you can to assure that this action will not be taken, *then* try to help the person explore and understand the meaning of the self-destructive thoughts and feelings. If it turns out that either "attention-getting" or "manipulation" is part of the client's motivation, work to help the person understand that, just as you would work to help them understand any other important wish or desire. I believe that many therapists and counselors who typically minimize the importance of suicidal ideation do so to help *themselves* deal with their own internal discomfort with the suicidal client.

Typically, I believe, it is *not* helpful when a counselor's values are brought into the helping relationship. I try to help clients decide, for example, whether or not *they* want a divorce, wish to confess that they stole the camera, or wish to change jobs—without even considering what my opinion might be. However, when a life is at stake, I do nothing to conceal my values. Here, I think the therapist's responsibilities are like those of a passerby who hears screams of "help me" coming from a burning or collapsed building. For a brief time, the passerby stops whatever he or she is doing (even if it happens to be psychotherapy), does whatever possible to help the endangered person, and then resumes the previous activity. I have heard some therapists say, "If a client I was seeing killed himself, it would not spoil my day," and "Her life is her responsibility; I can't do anything to stop her from killing herself if that's what she wants to do." Avoid becoming dispassionate and indifferent. Although you should not overestimate your responsibility for another's well-being, at times it can be an even bigger mistake to underestimate it.

I next will present some of the comments I have made that suicidal or self-destructive clients have found helpful. First, I have told such clients that it would be a mistake for them to kill anyone, themselves included. I sometimes say, "Would you try to stop me if you thought I were about to kill myself or someone else?" "Oh, yes, Dr. Brenner," is a common reply. I next say, "Well, that's how I feel about you right now." This simple turning of the tables clarifies just where I stand and reminds the client of the seriousness and finality of taking a human life. Such comments will be particularly helpful to those individuals who are trying to deny that they will murder a living, breathing human being if they commit suicide.

Next, I try to empathize with and accept whatever feelings underlie the suicidal thoughts. I let the person know that, in their situation, it is "OK" or "understandable" to feel trapped, angry, despondent, lonely. I sometimes say, "If I were in your shoes, I think I might feel miserable, too," and, "I'm very glad that you've shared these feelings with me, and I'm comfortable talking much more about them with you. But, I need to know that you won't act on these feelings." I reassure the person that, no matter how desperate he or she feels, there are bound to be better solutions than suicide—solutions that are not so final.

I say, on occasion, "You can kill yourself anytime, but, if you do that, you'd never get to try any of these other solutions that we've been discussing." Some people will detect a note of humor in this comment, and that is a good sign. People who have been able to look at me and smile have seemed less "lethal" than those who could not. However, additional assessment of a person's lethality usually will be in order. A rather accurate barometer of immediate danger is the extent to which the person has a specific plan and method available to end his or her life. The person who has a loaded revolver in his jacket pocket or a hunting knife under his pillow is much more apt to kill himself than an *equally miserable* individual who has not yet thought about or decided upon "a method" or who says, "I wish I were dead, but I could never do that to myself; I wish someone would do it for me." However, the person without a plan might still impulsively throw herself in front of a truck. Conversely, if a person with a knife or a gun gave it to you, the immediate threat might be reduced—but not eliminated.

After all is said and done, however, I have found that a simple, direct promise from the client is the best way both to assess lethality and to prevent a suicide. For example, I might say:

> We can talk about *anything* in here, and we can meet as often as you'd like. Your thoughts and feelings don't frighten me. But, I need to know that, no matter how badly you feel, you won't kill yourself—or even come close to it. If I feel that you might kill yourself between now and our next visit, I know that I won't be able to do my best work with you. I'd like you to promise me now that you won't kill yourself between now and our next visit.

Replies to this request will vary considerably and will, without a doubt, be important. At one extreme, some clients have said to me, "I'd never do *that*. When I said 'hurt myself,' I meant 'overeat.' And, although I've thought of suicide once or twice, I know I could never go through with it. Things could never get that bad." At the other extreme, a client may try to leave the room, may hide his or her head and sob for several minutes without saying a word, or may say, "Dr. Brenner, I couldn't make that promise to anyone right now." No matter what the client's response, I do not end a meeting until I am given, unambiguously, the promise or assurance I am looking for, regardless of how long it takes to get it.

A hurried, "OK, OK," while the client is looking at the floor, sounding irritated, will not do. And I request a promise to *see* me again, not phone me. I would never allow someone's life to hinge, possibly, on a telephone call; a telephone can be busy or out of order, or you might be out of reach when the person phones. I once sat for three hours with a woman before she could look me in the eye and sincerely say that she would appear for a visit with me on the following day. That happened many years ago, and she still writes me every year, never failing to remind me of how grateful she is that her life mattered to me that day—even though it did not matter to her.

I begin the *next* visit with an acutely suicidal client with a similar request for an assurance that he or she will appear for yet another visit. Gradually, it becomes easier for clients to make this commitment, and most will say, spontaneously, something like, "Dr. Brenner, we don't have to talk about this at the start of each meeting any more. I know I'm not going to kill myself in the near future. If I begin to have serious doubts again, I'll tell you."

I think this type of request for an assurance is a very good idea for at least three reasons. First, without such a promise, it would seem irrelevant to discuss with an acutely suicidal client, say, a broken romance, marital discord, or a drug problem. Why bother, if neither of you is sure that the client will return to continue the conversation? You are most likely to be helpful if you do not flinch from the most difficult issues. Second, this type of mutual, personal commitment is a dimension of effective counseling, regardless of a client's problems. To underscore this, I sometimes say, "What I am asking is that you promise not to precipitously abandon me in *any* way. And I'm willing to make that same promise to you." If you take the conversation in a direction that emphasizes your potential meaning to each other, it may become easier for a client to make emotional "contact" with you. Once this happens, the likelihood of suicide is lessened. Finally, your request and obvious willingness to become involved may encourage the person to reconsider some important questions. Some of these may be, "Am I as bad as I think I am?" "Will anyone ever care about me again?" "Will I ever be able to care about anyone else again?" "Will I always feel this miserable?"

Before concluding this discussion of suicide, I would like to make three more comments. First, I am not reluctant to be the "first one" to mention self-destruction or suicide. It is extraordinarily doubtful that you or I could plant such an idea in the mind of an individual who has not considered it.

We are not so powerful that the mere mention of a word can cause a death. Indeed, the likelihood of a suicide would be increased if a client was considering it but never got to discuss it with you. So, if a client does not mention suicide, but seems similar in important ways to previous clients who *have* mentioned it, I might say, "Do you ever feel so depressed (or 'lonely,' 'trapped,' 'angry,' or 'miserable') that you think of hurting yourself?" This question, which is most likely to be asked in an early session, leaves the client quite a bit of room. Consequently, the client's answer can be very helpful in your broader assessment of the client. For example, the person might say, with sincerity and confidence, "Oh, no, Dr. Brenner, I would never do that." Or, the client might say, "Yes," or "What do you mean, 'hurt' myself?" Once, in response to that question, a client rolled up her shirtsleeves and exposed dozens of self-inflicted scratches and cuts on her arms. Or, a client may respond by sobbing. When I am more confident that suicide is being considered, or when I am asked to clarify the word "hurt," I say, "Do you ever think of killing yourself," or "Are things so bad that you are thinking of suicide?" Some clients will be greatly relieved by your "breaking the ice" and mentioning what has been on their mind, but unspoken. Even if your "hunch" is incorrect, the client is apt to benefit from your example of candor and from your increased understanding that evolves from the conversation.

Second, no matter how depressed, despondent, or lifeless a suicidal client might seem, he or she is apt to be very angry and may not know it. This has not been true of *all* of the suicidal clients I have worked with, but it has been true of many of them. Many were discouraged forcefully and punished as children from expressing anger at anyone, especially their parents. They grew up "keeping it inside" and directing it toward the only "safe" person —themselves. Moreover, such people may feel guilty or tormented for feeling angry, hateful—even murderous—toward another person, and these feelings serve to reinforce the perception that *they* deserve to be hurt. I sometimes ask such a person, "Would it take much energy or anger for you to cut someone else's wrists, or for someone else to push you off a roof?" Almost always, the answer will be, "Yes." This can be the first step in helping a client realize that he or she might be feeling very angry inside. Then, over time, the client might become more willing to discuss and verbally express this anger in the safety of your office, and, finally, with friends and family. As this occurs, their suicidal thoughts and feelings will decrease proportionately.

Third, and finally, it is important to be alert to those clients who "tell" you indirectly or nonverbally that they are troubled by self-destructive impulses. I learned this from a client who always wore a bandanna that completely covered her scalp. I never thought to comment on it. Eventually, she said, "I'm surprised that you've never asked about my bandanna." As it turned out, this woman had pulled out just about every hair on her head, and, having run out of hair, she had begun to scratch herself here and there with a razor. I do not think it can ever be a mistake to make an innocuous comment about a conspicuous bandage or bruise or about a repeated, unusual mode of dress and to listen carefully for the client's reply. With three different clients, for example, I have inquired about long-sleeved shirts worn on successive, hot summer days. Twice, the clients were cutting their wrists and forearms with a razor. The other person had a very bothersome, embarrassing skin rash that covered most of her body. Although she had never told me about the rash, she had been told it was "psychological," and that was why she had entered psychotherapy.

WHEN YOU FEEL BEWILDERED

Regardless of how much experience you have had—or ever will have—there will be times when you will feel very confused and perplexed in the midst of a counseling session. You might feel that you have no idea what is going on or how to proceed. Your best efforts have led to dead ends. When this happens, I have found it best to use my uncertainty as an indication that something important—something I do not understand—is happening. If this ever happens to you, I recommend that, at that moment, you put a halt to whatever is going on and tell the client just how you feel. If you do not do this, matters may get worse, and the sessions that follow are not likely to be helpful. On the other hand, a client is apt to benefit from your expression of bewilderment.

Some clients, for example, will seem to resist your every effort to understand them. Even though they have come to you voluntarily, they seem determined to prevent progress at all costs. Any comment or inquiry leads to a dead end. All interpretations are, in one way or another, rejected, dismissed, or explained away. Attempts to empathize prove futile. The client will make a comment and may contradict it ten minutes or a week later. Counselors are frustrated by such people, and many are tempted to "label" the person as "schizoid," "passive–aggressive," "resistant," or "not motivated for treatment." Such labels may appear to provide the counselor an excuse to blame the lack of progress on the client, but they will "accomplish" little else.

I believe it is best to underscore the importance of these moments by letting the client know that I feel bewildered—even exasperated. I say something like:

> I have no idea what is going on right now. You seem to introduce a different topic every few minutes, almost as though you want to make sure that we don't explore any of them. You said earlier today that you thought this might

be our last session, but now you want to see me again this week. Sometimes you seem to start one sentence and finish another. I'm very confused. I'm lost. I can't hear anything else until you help me understand what is going on.

Needless to say, such remarks are bound to get the client's attention. Also, they are apt to underscore the client's responsibility in the relationship and to take the conversation in a new direction. Such a comment, along with your insistence that the client respond to it, sometimes will be the necessary first step of effective therapy. You may learn, for example, that the client dislikes or does not trust you and wants to make sure that you do not learn too much. Or, perhaps the client wants to see how honest *you* are willing to be. Perhaps you will learn that the client does not want to come to you at all, but is doing so under pressure from an employer or family member. You may learn that you have assessed the client incorrectly and that he or she has a thought disorder and is not able to partake in a prolonged, coherent conversation. In short, your confusion is apt to be a reflection of confusion, doubt, or some other important process operating within the client. Your failure to comment on your confusion would be a disservice to the client.

Next, I wish to discuss the client who comes to you with a presenting problem that either is very new to you or is very similar to the problem of former clients with whom you have not been your most effective. In these instances, I say something like this:

Of course, no two people are the same, but I want you to know that I haven't yet worked with a person who has had a problem quite like the one you've just described. (Or, "Of course, no two people are the same, but I want you to know that, in the past, I have not been as helpful as I would have liked with clients who have had problems similar to yours.") That's a comment about *me* and the experiences *I've* had—not about you. If you'd like, we can plan to meet regularly, and, with your permission, I will discuss our meetings with a colleague who has worked extensively and successfully with people similar to you. Or, I'm equally willing to tell you this person's name and to help arrange for you to start seeing her directly instead of me.

It is important to know your limits and, when appropriate, to tell a client about them. However, some clients will not care the least bit about your limitations or prior experiences. For example, you recently may have been very helpful to a close friend of the client. The friend may have recommended you, and the client may be unwilling to see anyone but yourself, regardless of all other considerations. I think it is *far* better to see such a person—provided that consultation or supervision is available—than to refer them and, possibly, deny them a counseling relationship.

In other words, even if you do not feel very confident with a certain person, it may still be best that you see that person. Do not try to conceal from a client an area of inexperience. On the other hand, do not avoid automatically every "new" type of person that comes along or the person who is similar to your most miserable failure. Be candid with each client. When appropriate, work to stretch your abilities, as long as you have a qualified consultant or supervisor available. By doing so, gradually, you will become increasingly qualified to serve a broader range of clients.

Sometimes you may feel bewildered because a client has so *many* problems, even though no one of them may be new to you. For example, I once had a first meeting with a young man, who, during the previous week had received a rejection letter from the last possible graduate school that might admit him, had been accused formally of plagiarism, had been told that his "girlfriend" of more than one year did not want to go out with him any longer, and had learned of the death of his father. A woman once came to me because, within a week's time her best friend killed herself, another very good friend "joined a fanatical commune and might as well be dead," a man she was romantically interested in told her he was "gay," her father was hospitalized with terminal cancer, and her roommate told her that she was moving out because the client was so "gloomy."

More than most clients, such people are at an important crossroad in their life. They are apt to feel overwhelmed—even desperate—and to need your prompt encouragement and understanding. The fact that you are a stranger will not matter; the client may see you as his or her last hope. In such situations, this is what I say:

> You've had an *incredible* amount of misfortune recently. It almost overwhelms me just to hear about it, so I can imagine how you must feel. But, I sense that you are a very strong person, and still hopeful, or you probably wouldn't be here right now. And, I'm hopeful and optimistic about you. There's so much happening, it's hard to know where to begin. But, let's start somewhere. What would you like to talk about first?

If you then make progress together on any one of the problems, the client is apt to believe that he or she has "come to the right place" and that, together, you can cope with all of the problems. Empathy and support are very important with such clients; but, I think some immediate progress is needed, too, to help lift the burden.

Chapter 7
Trust, Privilege, and Confidentiality

> The right of the people to be secure in their persons,
> houses, papers and effects against unreasonable
> searches and seizures, shall not be violated. . . .
> —Fourth Amendment, United
> States Constitution

> About 25 years ago, a child we were examining at a
> court psychiatric clinic expressed angry, homicidal
> kinds of thinking. His mother was told by one of
> the examiners, and she duly punished him. A decade
> later he assassinated the President of the United
> States.
> —Max Siegel, 1976, p. 1.

It is important to keep in mind that clients inevitably will be involved in a number of complex, ongoing relationships. In all likelihood, there will be at least one additional person very interested in the work you do with each and every client you see. In fact, many clients who come to you will do so precisely because they are having difficulty getting along with others, some of whom are apt to want to speak with you about the client. These requests might come, for example, from a spouse, parent, close friend, professional colleagues, or from an attorney, insurance company, or employer. Some third party requests will seem very informal, such as "My son told me he's seeing you and that he likes it a lot. Are things going O.K.?" Or, they might be very formal and official, such as a witnessed release of information form from a mental health department, or a subpoena. Usually, clients are likely to both know of and be influenced by your involvement with third parties.

The term, "third party," can be defined as "anyone who presents himself or is presented by the patient or by the therapist as having interests, rights, prerogatives or concerns regarding the patient [Wohl, 1974, p. 530]." The nature of your involvement with third parties often will be an important ingredient in the counseling relationship. At times it will be very helpful if you talk with someone about a client. As a result, the client's relationship with you, the third party, or both might be improved. If handled improperly, however, the client may find your interaction with another person to be unsettling—even devastating. It could destroy the counseling relationship, with the client feeling betrayed.

It is especially difficult to work with a third party when there is not a specific request from the client that you share information with that person. For example, the third party involvement inherent in any form of therapy in which there are more than two people directly involved often is overlooked. In group or family counseling, for example, in which a number of people simultaneously hear a client's comments, guidelines regarding privacy often are misunderstood or absent altogether. Further, in either individual or group counseling, there may be a time when *you* want to involve a third party in some way, even though the client may object to your doing so.

It is important that you have a framework for working with third parties who might approach you, whom you might want to approach, or who might obtain information firsthand in a group. Otherwise, because of the variety and complexity of third party involvements, you might be tempted to treat them superficially or capriciously and consequently overlook issues at the heart and soul of therapy. For example, at what point, if any, would you inform a third party of an impending crime that a client, who insists that you remain silent, tells you about? Or, less dramatically, what would you do if the parents of a financially-dependent adolescent client asked you for information, and the client insisted that you "keep everything confidential"? The parents might refuse to pay for counseling if you did not answer their questions, and the son or daughter might refuse to continue if you did. You might be able to sidestep this problem by offering the client a reduced fee, but what if you could not afford to do so, or what if the client was too proud to accept it? Finally, what would you do if the director of the agency at which you worked requested some information about a client, and the client did not want it revealed?

Other serious problems can arise from unnoticed, routine procedures. For example, professional groups encourage therapists to keep written records of meetings with clients, and laws in many states require that such records be kept and maintained, sometimes for many years after you "terminate" with a client. Abuses of these records, or at least an undesired dissemination of information, can occur because a number of people (e.g., colleagues in your office, consultants, clerks, secretaries) may have ready access to these records. Moreover, records are sometimes kept in an unlocked file, or in a locked file that can be opened with a widely available, standard key. Siegel (1979) has noted the "inadequate security of client and patient records in the offices of psychologists, psychiatrists, psychiatric social workers, and other mental health workers [p. 17]."

The countless issues and questions that can arise need to be answered case by case, working with each client, exploring the possibilities. There are no simple rules. However, it is possible to identify the components of a framework for making the decisions and answering the questions that will arise. These components are discussed in the following three sections: Trust, Privilege, and Confidentiality; Duty to Warn, and Third Party Intrusions.

TRUST, PRIVILEGE, AND CONFIDENTIALITY

An effective therapeutic relationship is based on a foundation of trust. Trust has been described as the "cornerstone" of psychotherapy and counseling (e.g., Plotkin, 1978; Slovenko, 1976). By definition, a client who trusts you will have faith and confidence in your good intentions, integrity, judgment, and sincerity. Such a client will be willing to disclose and discuss previously hidden thoughts and feelings (Cousins, 1979; Jourard, 1971; Meares, 1980; Rynearson, 1978). To the degree that trust is absent, clients are apt to be suspicious, withholding, evasive, and unwilling to discuss the private thoughts and feelings that led them to you.

To a limited degree, trust is objective, based on criteria such as your training, professional degree, licenses, and certificates. Because of this, some clients enter a therapeutic relationship with the mistaken belief that their privacy is "automatically" protected. However, this type of naive belief in the trustworthiness of therapists is becoming increasingly rare as reports of litigation, professional misconduct, and carelessness become increasingly common. Indeed, people can be found who—despite the apparent need—refuse to enter a therapeutic relationship because they are certain that therapists cannot be trusted and will not respect their privacy.

More than ever before, you will have to earn the trust of each client you see. To a large degree, clients are apt to trust you if you treat effectively the issues discussed in the previous six chapters. Do you have the personal qualities that most people find desirable in counselors? Are you responsive to the questions and concerns that the client brings to the first meeting? Do you promptly seek to identify a client's strengths? Do you disregard a client's easily observable physical characteristics? Do you consider psychoactive medication only as a last resort? Are you responsive and authentic at crucial, one-of-a-kind moments? If you answer to these questions is "yes," you will have gone a long way in earning a client's trust.

In addition, however, you must be committed to protecting a client's privacy whenever possible. If an informed client wants you to speak with someone, so be it. But, whenever there is doubt or reluctance—and usually there will be—you should do everything possible to protect the privacy of each client. Regardless of all else, trust, the *sine qua non* of effective therapy, will not develop if you fail to do this. Moreover, as you work to protect a client's privacy, you simultaneously will be demonstrating your trustworthiness.

Trust follows from a resolute, personal commitment to protect the privacy of your conversations with each client. This personal commitment is perhaps the ultimate, unique feature of the professional, effective, helping relationship. It may be the single most important quality you have to offer each client. Regardless of all else, if you betray a client's trust, he or she likely will know it, and you will have failed. Moreover, in addition to the direct harm done to the client, your reputation (and thus your ability to help others) can suffer greatly from the complaints and bitterness of one client whose trust was betrayed and whose words will outweigh the silent satisfaction of many. Conversely, if you are trustworthy and respect clients' privacy, they, at the very least, will be unlikely to have regrets about their decision to see you. They will continue to see professional counselors and therapists as potential sources of help to themselves and others.

Neither laws nor ethical codes can protect a client's confidences. Only you can. To clarify this point, I next will discuss the terms "privilege" and "confidentiality." Privilege, despite its definition, offers clients little protection. It is defined as "the legal right which exists by statute and which protects the client from having his confidences revealed publicly in the witness stand during legal proceedings without his permission (Shah, 1969, p. 57)." Since privilege applies only to legal proceedings, it would be less than honest to encourage clients to believe that their privacy is protected by legal privileges in the day-to-day third party involvements that might arise.

Whether or not a client's comments to you are considered privileged by the courts depends upon the ever-changing state laws in force at the time for your particular profession. Moreover, state and federal statutes, laws, and regulations often do not agree, and may even directly contradict each other (Everstine, Everstine, Heymann, True, Frey, Johnson, & Seiden, 1980). Privilege rarely provides shelter, even to those clients who appear to be "protected" by it.

> The history of the privilege concept . . . reveals that it has not been very much
> of a shield in the armamentarium of the healing arts. When push has come to

shove, the privilege has ended up not shielding very much, if anything. It is like the warranty where the bold print giveth and the fine print taketh away. Among the hundreds of cases concerning medical privilege there is apparently not one reported decision (matrimonial actions excepted) in which a physician or psychotherapist, when called to testify, was allowed to keep silent on the basis of the privilege [Slovenko, 1977, p. 412].

Paradoxically, the "privileged" nature of a relationship is more likely to remain intact if there are *no* laws protecting it. "Legislation often results in the very opposite of what it ordains [Slovenko, 1977, p. 428]." For example, although there is no legal privilege between employer and secretary, a secretary never has been forced to testify in court against an employer. Secretaries have been subpoenaed (as was Rose Mary Woods against Richard Nixon), but to no avail. Slovenko (1977) has concluded that if an employer-secretary privilege were enacted, it "would soon be punctured with exceptions and limitations [p. 428]." Privilege is a legal concept of dubious value. Although a number of clients may believe that the privacy of their relationship with you is legally protected, it is not.

Where privilege is a legal concept, confidentiality, as it applies to psychotherapists and counselors, "relates to matters of professional ethics [Shah, 1969, p. 57]." Since confidentiality is an ethical concept, not a legal one, the confidentiality of helping relationships has found little—if any—legal protection. Members of the Committee on Privacy and Confidentiality of the California State Psychological Association recently concluded that "in respect to psychotherapy, little confidentiality exists. . . . Many citizens have the illusion of being protected by federal law" when, in fact, they are not (Everstine et al., 1980, p. 838).

An ethical code or professional organization cannot protect a client's confidentiality. Only the therapist or counselor can. Virtually all of the helping professions include unambiguous statements in their ethical codes regarding the necessity of confidentiality in therapeutic and counseling relationships; an exception is to be made only when life (or in some cases, property) is in danger. Nonetheless, within each professional group, there is much variation. Some therapists protect a client's privacy as much as their own or that of a loved one. Others, however, do not respect clients' confidences and seem willing to speak with third parties at almost any opportunity. People hear stories—accurate ones—regarding the frequency with which professionals talk with each other, without clients' knowledge or consent, about identified clients, even if their involvement with that person is tangential or nonexistent. Other counselors obey the letter but not the spirit of their ethical code. For example, some "ask" mentally deficient citizens or very young children to sign blanket, "informed" consent forms granting the release of confidential information. Such stories may be the exception, not the rule. But, they are reason enough for many to avoid therapists and counselors. Many of us have been careless with the ethical principle of confidentiality, and the public knows it. And, those clients who are aware of professional ethical boards and conduct review committees are inclined to see them as groups that protect the professional—not the consumer.

In summary, a client's privacy will be protected rarely if ever by law or an ethical code. It is up to you—no one else—to protect the privacy of each client. If you do not offer such protection, you will not be trusted, and your effectiveness will be limited severely.

Oftentimes, especially with clients that you see for more than two or three visits, it will be important to discuss some of these issues. Many clients will care a great deal about the extent to which their relationship with you is private. I do not mean to suggest that, with every client whom you see for more than a few visits, you initiate a prolonged discussion of trust, privilege, and confidentiality. On the other hand, it would be equally inappropriate to encourage clients to think that their privacy is legally or professionally protected when in fact it is not. A client might be quite distressed to learn at, say, the tenth meeting with you, that you can imagine a situation in which state law, your ethical code, or your conscience might dictate that you involve a third party in your relationship. Every client is different, and I believe it is best to decide the extent to which you discuss these matters on a case by case basis. Whenever there is doubt as to how much to discuss trust, privilege, and confidentiality with a client, I think it is best to err on the side of saying too much rather than not enough.

I have found that, almost invariably, such discussions heighten clients' understanding of their relationship with me. After a client realizes that it is I, not ethical codes or laws, who protect his or her privacy, our relationship often becomes more personal, more "real." Then, clients are more able to see the immediate relevance of our relationship to their outside lives. On the other hand, this knowledge might frighten some clients who might then choose not to disclose certain thoughts or feelings or to discontinue the visits altogether. Nonetheless, I think this is better than having a client share private thoughts and feelings prematurely with a false sense of security.

There is certain information that should be shared with all clients, either verbally or via a printed sheet that is given to them at or before the first meeting. If you routinely confer with colleagues, for example, or if secretaries type notes on your visits, clients should know that "confidentiality" means confidentiality within the immediate staff of the office in which you work. Reassurance should be provided that you would share information with a co-worker only after you were as sure of that person's discretion as you are of your own. Or, with a particular client, if you anticipate the involvement of a third party, try to discuss this possibility before it happens—not after. This might occur when someone other than the client pays the bills for a client's visits with you, or when a client has committed, or intends to commit, a crime.

Also, clients should know of your legal obligations as a counselor. For example, there is a law in New York State requiring guidance counselors to report or have a designee report all instances of child abuse that they learn about in counseling sessions. Following is an example of the type of statement regarding your legal obligations that you might provide to clients (Everstine et al., 1980):

> You should . . . know that there are certain situations in which, as a psychotherapist, I am required *by law* to reveal information obtained during therapy to other persons or agencies—*without your permission*. Also, I am not required to inform you of my actions in this regard. These situations are as follows: (a) If you threaten grave bodily harm or death to another person, I am required by law to inform the intended victim and appropriate law enforcement agencies; (b) if a court of law issues a legitimate subpoena, I am required by law to provide the information specifically described in the subpoena; (c) if you are in therapy or being tested by order of a court of law, the results of the treatment or tests ordered must be revealed to the court [pp. 832–833].

Such a statement will be irrelevant to most clients. But, with, say, a homicidal client, or one involved in complex legal proceedings—the type of person who might be most in need of your services—your effectiveness is apt to be determined in large part by whether or not you present and discuss such a statement. In short, you make the relationship potentially more valuable to the extent that you help a client understand the context in which it occurs. Clients should know both their rights and your obligations. As a result, most clients will experience the relationship for what it is, a professional one but also a personal one in which you will respect the client's privacy whenever possible. Paradoxically, you will be demonstrating your integrity and trustworthiness by helping clients realize that their relationship with you cannot exist totally separate from society's laws.

DUTY TO WARN

Next, I will discuss how to proceed when you decide on your own to involve a third party or when you legally are obligated to do so. Although such moments are apt to arise only once, twice, or not at all in your career, it is important to be prepared. Someone's life may depend on your comments or actions.

Regardless of the situation—even if a life is at stake—I believe it is best to work *with* and *for* the client whenever possible. Menninger (1960) has stated, "If a patient tells a doctor in confidence that he has brought a time bomb into the hospital and hidden it under the bed of one of the patients, it would be a strange doctor indeed who would feel that this professional confidence should not be violated [p. 36]." I disagree. I think it would be better to look first for alternatives that would both remove the threat of the bomb and strengthen (or at least preserve) your relationship with a client who needs help desperately. For example, if time permitted, the *client* might be willing to notify the proper authorities in your presence, or give you permission to take responsible action, which would not necessarily include disclosing his name. A hasty violation of confidentiality may not be the ethical, responsible action to take, even when life is in immediate danger. For example, the client's cooperation may be needed to disarm or remove the bomb or to say exactly where it is. Such cooperation is not apt to be forthcoming after you have talked with others about the client against his wishes.

Virtually all situations will have a number of possibly effective options available to the counselor *before* the decision is made to violate confidentiality (Lane & Spruill, 1980). If, for example, a client tells you that she plans to kill someone, you might try to obtain her assurance that she will not do so "between now and our next meeting" (in the manner described in the previous chapter's discussion of the suicidal client). Or, you might ask the client if *she*—rather than you—would tell others voluntarily about her intention. Or, you might warn the police and potential victim without revealing the name of the client.

Prompt, effective, responsible action can be taken without revealing a client's name. Conversely, if you do reveal the client's name against his wishes, the only thing you can be sure of is that the client will not see you—or probably anyone else—voluntarily in therapy again. Furthermore, violation of confidentiality can amount to abandoning a client who needs your help desperately. Siegel (1976) writes:

> The young, angry adolescent who confides in me that he has planted an explosive device in the teacher's (or principal's or whatever) automobile will not be helped by my interceding and violating this confidence. Almost 100% of the time, I have been able to get the adolescent, who is really very depressed underneath it all, to remove the danger himself—and if not, to grant me permission to have it moved without revealing my source. . . . In no case would I stand by, in the absence of permission from the client, and permit injury, disease or death—but in no case would I break confidence. . . . As I reflect over my 35 years in clnical psychology, I am all the more convinced that my failures were most often associated with an absence of mutual respect and trust, and my successes with complete, unequivocal acceptance and trust [p. 1].

In short, when someone's life is threatened, if you do what is best for the client, you are likely to be doing what is best for the potential victim. To the extent that you alienate the client—even if it is to contact the police—you jeopardize the well-being of the potential victim. Virtually every assassin or would-be assassin of a public figure in the last two decades has been described as "a former mental patient." To a one, these people, at one point in their lives before committing murder, reached out to a counselor who failed to remain the client's ally.

Any discussion of this nature must consider the widely cited case of *Tarasoff* v. *Board of Regents of the University of California*, which many believe will have nationwide implications. Everstine et al. (1980) provide a brief account of what happened:

> On August 20, 1969, a man named Prosenjit Poddar, who was a voluntary outpatient at Cowell Memorial Hospital on the Berkeley campus, informed his therapist, a psychologist, that he was planning to kill a young woman. Poddar did not name the woman, but as established later, the psychologist could easily have inferred who she was. The murder was to be carried out when the woman returned to Berkeley from her summer vacation.
>
> Following this session, the psychologist telephoned the campus police to ask them to observe Poddar for possible hospitalization as a person who was "dangerous to himself or others"; he then wrote a letter, containing a formal request for assistance, to the chief of the campus police. The campus officers took Poddar into custody for the purpose of questioning, but later released him when he gave evidence of being "rational." Soon afterward the psychologist's supervisor, Director of the Department of Psychiatry at Cowell Hospital, asked the campus police to return the psychologist's letter, ordered that the letter and therapy notes that had been made in Poddar's case be destroyed, and directed that no further action be taken to hospitalize Poddar. No warning was given either to the intended victim or to her parents. The client, naturally enough, did not resume his therapy.
>
> On October 27, 1969, Prosenjit Poddar killed Tatiana Tarasoff. The victim's parents filed suit against the Board of Regents of the university, several employees of Cowell Hospital, and the chief of the campus police plus four of his officers. A lower court dismissed the suit, the parents appealed, and the California Supreme Court upheld the appeal in 1974 and reaffirmed its decision in 1976. In July 1977, the suit was settled out of court and the Tarasoff family received a substantial award [p. 835].

Specifically, the California Supreme Court mandated the duty that:

> When a therapist determines, or pursuant to the standards of his profession should determine, that his patient presents a serious danger of violence to another, he incurs an obligation to use reasonable care to protect the intended victim against such danger. The discharge of this duty may require the therapist to take one or more of various steps, depending upon the nature of the case. Thus it may call for him to warn the intended victim or others likely

to apprise the victim of the danger, to notify the police, or to take whatever other steps are reasonably necessary under the cirumstances [Slovenko, 1977, pp. 425–426].

Some (e.g., Roth & Meisel, 1977) have been very critical of this decision and believe that it marks the beginning of a broad erosion of therapeutic relationships, especially with seriously troubled clients who are most in need of such a relationship. Further, the court has been accused of directing therapists to predict "dangerousness" accurately and of imposing on therapists a "duty to warn" or impending danger. Mistakenly, some have equated this duty with the violation of confidentiality.

However, I believe that the Tarasoff ruling is a good one and that it is entirely consistent with the counseling approach being advocated here. For example, the ruling does *not* require that the therapist predict "dangerousness." Rather, it requires that the therapist act to "protect the intended victim." These two are different. There are a number of ways in which you can see to it that a threatened person is protected *without* ascertaining how dangerous is the individual making the threats. Also, no mention is made in the ruling that the name of the "dangerous" client be disclosed. "Duty to warn" neither necessitates nor implies violation of confidentiality. The Tarasoff ruling calls for nothing more than—but, nothing less than—competent, professional judgment and action.

Finally, it is important to note that Poddar killed Tarasoff more than two months after he first told the psychologist of his plans. There was plenty of time for thought and discussion. Rarely, if ever, will it help either the client or the potential victim if you make a sudden move that will alienate the client. Try to find an alternative that will both protect the potential victim and solidify your relationship with the client. The following suggestions (Roth & Meisel, 1977) are directed toward physicians but are applicable to all therapists and counselors.

Even when danger seems imminent there are a number of social or environmental manipulations which may be agreed upon by the doctor and patient that reduce the patient's dangerousness without compromising confidentiality. For example, other persons may be brought into the therapy or it may be insisted that the patient rid himself of lethal weapons.

Some patients, when apprised of the psychiatrist's fears and necessity to act to protect others, are willing to warn potential victims or permit others to warn them about the patient's fears, anger, and recent turmoil. When disclosing information about the patient to others, the physician must attempt to obtain the patient's permission to do so and should reveal the disturbing information about the patient in his presence.

The psychiatrist's need to act should always be assessed in light of the impact of the proposed intervention on future therapy with the patient and in light of the likelihood of success in preventing violence. If the probability of compromising future therapy is great and/or if the likelihood of the success of the intervention is slight, the psychiatrist may prefer to rely on the odds and to hope for the best, rather than warning a potential victim or attempting to hospitalize the patient involuntarily [p. 511].

THIRD PARTY INTRUSIONS

Most occasions that require your making a decision with a client about a third party will be much less dramatic than those discussed immediately above. Nonetheless, to the extent that you fail to put the client's interests and wishes first, you will limit your effectiveness. Regardless of the circumstances, it will be best to discuss the third party (e.g., a relative, an insurance company, an employer) with the client before making any decision about releasing information. By doing so, you are most likely to arrive at a decision that will be best for the client. Further, such a discussion may help the client sort out and understand his or her feelings regarding the third party involvement.

The various types of third party involvements will be discussed under three headings: *Record Keeping*, *Third Party Payment*, and *Third Parties with a Personal Interest*.

Record Keeping

Do not overlook the importance of the written records that you keep that summarize the work you do with each client. Typically, these records will be the primary source of any information that is shared with a third party. As mentioned above, most professional groups—and many state laws—require that written records be kept. These records might inadvertently become a source of information to someone; any written document can be lost, mislaid, or stolen. And, as Hirsh (1979) points out, any record that you keep has the potential to become a legal document—either with or without your approval. Davis (1979), for example, describes an instance in which a therapist's records were subpoenaed: the prosecuting attorney "appeared at the office of the clinical psychologist and after displaying the warrant, wheeled a photocopying machine into the file room [p. 19]" and copied the information he was looking for. He copied many irrelevant documents in the process, to make sure that the relevant information would be included.

Because of the possible abuses of written records, some therapists maintain "whitewashed" records that contain only minimal information (e.g., the client's first name, last name or initial, and the dates of each meeting). By keeping this type of record, a therapist satisfies the letter of the law only. This approach is epitomized in a group therapist's comments to Slovenko

(1977): "Primarily I keep records of who was there and maybe a couple of sentences about the mood of the group. I used to keep elaborate notes. I used to tape. I stopped doing that because of legal things. I don't want to have a lot of records [p. 460]." It is worth noting that therapists are not alone in their reluctance to maintain wholly accurate records. According to Slovenko (1977), "Earl Long, when governor of Louisiana, said to Troy Middleton, President of Louisiana State University, 'I'll be writing you a lot of letters. Pay no attention to them. That's for the record. If I ever need anything, I'll telephone.'"

Although there are risks associated with keeping clear, accurate, and descriptive records, I think it is best to do so. On the other hand, a hastily prepared note, sprinkled with pejorative terms and enigmatic phrases might just as well not be written. I try to prepare a one or two paragraph note after each meeting that contains the client's name, the date, relevant problems and difficulties, and progress made toward identified goals. This type of record can be a crucial ingredient in effective counseling, especially if a client moves, is referred to someone else, or is seen by you over a long period of time.

For example, a particular client came to me for three successive years on exactly the same day in October. He complained of "depression," and, in each of the first two years, he did not return for a second visit. (I mistakenly considered the date of his second visit as a "coincidence.") At our third visit, I pointed this pattern out to him and asked if the date of the visit had special significance in his life. He was quite surprised at my question and did not even remember his first visit with me, exactly two years previously. This date turned out to be the anniversary of his father's death, an event that the client had never mentioned to me previously. During the following weeks, we had a number of very productive meetings, and the young man's reaction to his father's death was the main topic of conversation each time. If we all maintained and read our records more carefully, I believe stories of this nature would be more common.

Inevitably, certain clients will reveal to you something that is potentially damaging to them—something that they do not want anyone else to know. Should this information be put in the record? Here, Zaro, Barach, Nedelman, and Dreiblatt (1978) have excellent advice:

> A client may disclose information that he or she has acted illegally, immorally, or indiscreetly, but these actions have no relevance or bearing on the client's present life or on therapeutic issues. An example of this situation would be a mental health professional you are seeing in therapy who tells you that at one time he or she had sexual relations with a client. This fact is irrelevant to your client's reasons for entering therapy, and if it became known to members of the professional community it would have detrimental consequences. What

should you include in your records about this incident? As a general rule, we believe that you have a higher responsibility to protect your client from inadvertent exposure to damaging information than to have totally complete records. When you are faced with decisions about what to include in your written records, we believe a useful guide is whether the client would suffer *unnecessarily* if the records somehow come into the wrong hands [pp. 160–161].

If the information is relevant to the client's present life or to current therapeutic issues, include it in the record—discreetly—in a manner in which you would want your records maintained if you went to a therapist. If the information appears to have little or no relevance to the work you are doing with the client, it would probably be best to leave it out of the record.

Third Party Payment

Wohl (1974) notes the "ancient tradition that he who pays for services requires rights with respect to those services even if the service is not rendered directly to him [p. 536]." Usually, insurance companies are spotlighted in discussions of "third party payment," but such payers can be spouses, parents, or others who might, sooner or later, request access to certain information that you have. Traditionally, *any* third party involvement has been viewed as a contamination of the therapeutic relationship. "Freud recommended as a basic condition of psychotherapy the relative independence of the patient, so that therapy could function outside of environmental pressure [Standal & Corsini, 1959, p. 190]." Szasz (1965), who agrees with Freud on little else, believes that effective therapy requires that therapist and client freely agree to a contract with each other without third party involvement. However, as increasing numbers of highly visible insurance companies pay for the services of therapists and counselors, it has become virtually impossible to avoid consideration of third party payers. Such involvement has been debated on both theoretical and practical grounds (Albee, 1977a, 1977b; Derner, 1977a, 1977b) but is doubtless here to stay.

Oftentimes, it will be best to talk with the client about the third party who is paying for part or all of the service you are providing. Clients will appreciate your helping them think through issues that are new to them but not to you. For example, are forms sent to the insurance company directly, or via their employer? Does the client realize that once he or she authorizes you to release information to a third party—even a third party payer—it becomes much more difficult to withhold information from the courts (Slovenko, 1977)? Does the client realize that you have no control over the discretion with which the third party will treat the information that you send to them?

Discussion of these and similar questions can be very helpful to a client. Clarification of issues related to confidentiality and independence are apt to help the client understand the therapeutic relationship more fully. It also can bring you and the client closer together and set the stage for an honest relationship in which important matters are discussed as they arise.

It is equally important to be honest with insurance companies or any other third party payer. When third party payment is available, avoid any questionable alteration of the nature or frequency of your meetings with clients. For example, if it is best to see family members together, do not see them individually because "the insurance company will pay for it." Similarly, avoid seeing anyone with insurance coverage for more visits than you would have seen that person if such coverage were not available. Such practices might increase your short-term income, but they are even *more* likely to interfere with communication among members of a family or to invite clients to depend on you unnecessarily. Moreover, such an approach, sooner or later, will harm seriously both your reputation and that of your profession.

Third Parties with a Personal Interest

In a sense, it is easiest to make decisions about a third party who might become personally involved in the counseling relationship. Examples here are a client's spouse who asks if there is anything he or she can or should be doing to help, or a parent who phones you to discuss a son or daughter. On these occasions, if the client asks you to speak with the third party, you might ask the client something like, "How would it help you if I speak with your wife on the telephone?" The ensuing discussion might teach the client something new. Perhaps, for example, the client is more dependent on his wife than he led you to believe when he requested that he see you without her. Perhaps the client wants you to say something to his wife, or perhaps he wants you to speak with her so that he might ask your opinion of her. In short, important things often are going on behind the scenes when either a client or a third party asks you to talk with someone else about the client.

After the request is understood, and if both you and the client think it is best that you speak with the third party, you can do so with confidence. If, on the other hand, you believe that third party involvement will interfere with therapy, explain your reservations to the client and discuss them until a decision is reached.

If a third party contacts me before I have discussed that individual with the client, I say—except in the most extreme circumstances—that I will discuss a client with a third person only at the client's request. Such a comment can be made without even acknowledging that I know the client. I would then talk with the client about the third party request at our next meeting.

Third party involvements in any form of group therapy are often overlooked. Here, six or eight "third parties" might hear a client's comments simultaneously. Indeed, some therapists avoid group work primarily because the third party issues raised are so complex. I think this unfortunate, since many clients are best served by a group. Moreover, the problems differ in number rather than kind; helpers who fail to face third party involvements in group therapy are apt to be doing so in individual therapy as well.

It can be very helpful to discuss privacy at the first meeting of any group that you lead or facilitate. At such a meeting, I refer to group members' responsibility to each other and indicate that I will not discuss the group with anyone, except during actual group meetings. I also mention that group members are not protected by legal privilege because they are not considered professionals by the courts (Meyer & Smith, 1977, p. 643). Inevitably, these comments lead group members to discuss confidentiality and privacy, to begin to establish shared ground rules, and to talk honestly with each other about matters of immediate concern. Thus, as in individual therapy, they begin to realize almost immediately that the experience will be helpful only if those directly involved discuss the concerns that brought them together in a climate of mutual respect and trust.

Coda

Intentionally, the termination visit has not been discussed in any detail in this book. When used in the context of an effective helping relationship, the word "termination" has an inappropriate finality to it. If you are effective, your relationship with clients and the changes they made with your help will remain important to them long after the "final" visit. Moreover, you often will not know which visit is the last. Any visit, including the first, may also be the last. Now and then, someone whom you anticipate seeing many times will miss or cancel an appointment and make no other. Some people will announce at the very end of a meeting that they want to stop seeing you and simultaneously make it clear that they do not want to discuss the decision in any detail. Still others, with whom you think you have terminated, unexpectedly will request to see you again or will send an annual card or letter, which will reflect your continuing importance.

Do your best work in each and every meeting, respect clients' rights to come and go as they please, and you will have a lasting influence on many people who come to you for help. Further, they likely will consider seeing you again—or will be reassured by the knowledge that they may if they wish—if life's stresses become too great.

Similarly, I hope that this book will be a continuing resource to you. If, for example, you gradually become a bit careless about clients' privacy, or if you rely increasingly on pejorative terms of minimal reliability and validity, I hope that you will think of this book as a reference point—a place to return to privately regain perspective.

References

Adams, H. Toward a dialectical approach to counseling. *Journal of Humanistic Psychology*, 1977, *17*, 57-67.

Adams, S. & Orgel, M. *Through the mental health maze*. Washington, D.C.: Health Research Group, 1975.

Ahn Toupin, E. S. Counseling Asians: Psychotherapy in the context of racism and Asian-American history. *American Journal of Orthopsychiatry*, 1980, *50*, 76-86.

Alagna, F. J., Sheryle, J. W., Fisher, J. D., & Wicas, E. A. Evaluative reaction to touch in a counseling interview. *Journal of Counseling Psychology*, 1979, *26*, 465-472.

Albee, G. W. Problems in living are not sicknesses: Psychotherapy should not be covered under national health insurance. *The Clinical Psychologist*, Spring 1977, *30*, 5-6. (a)

Albee, G. W. Silver and golden comments on Dr. Derner. *The Clinical Psychologist*, Spring 1977, *30*, 7-8; 13. (b)

Albin, R. Psychotherapy: Keeping it short. *APA Monitor*, May 1980, pp. 6-7.

Allport, G. W. *The Nature of prejudice*. Reading, Mass.: Addison-Wesley, 1954.

Allyon, T., Layman, D., & Kandel, H. J. A behavioral-educational alternative to drug control of hyperactive children. *Journal of Applied Behavior Analysis*, 1975, *8*, 141-144.

American Psychiatric Association. *Diagnostic and statistical manual of mental disorders* (3rd ed.) Washington, D.C.: American Psychiatric Association, 1980.

Anderson, J. G. Growth groups and alienation: A comparative study of Rogerian encounter, self-directed encounter and gestalt. *Group and Organization Studies*, 1978, *3*, 85-107.

Andrade, E. H. *An approach to modern physics*. Garden City, N.Y.: Doubleday, 1956.

Applebaum, S. A. To define and decipher the borderline syndrome. *Psychotherapy: Theory, Research and Practice*, 1979, *16*, 364-370.

Armstrong, H. E., Jr., & Booth, C. An educational program for obesity management: Preliminary report. *Psychotherapy: Theory, Research and Practice*, 1979, *16*, 286-291.

Beier, E. G. *The silent language of psychotherapy*. Chicago: Aldine, 1966.

Bergman, H., Borg, S., & Holm, L. Neuropsychological impairment and exclusive use of sedatives or hypnotics. *American Journal of Psychiatry*, 1980, *137*, 215-217.

Berman, J. Counseling skills used by black and white male and female counselors. *Journal of Counseling Psychology*, 1979, *26*, 81-84.

Berne, E. *Transactional analysis in psychotherapy*. New York: Grove Press, 1961.

Blazer, D., & Williams, C. D. Epidemiology of dysphoria and depression in an elderly population. *American Journal of Psychiatry*, 1980, *137*, 439-444.

Bloch, D. *"So the witch won't eat me": Fantasy and the child's fear of infanticide*. Boston: Houghton Mifflin, 1978.

Blumenthal, M. D., & Davie, J. W. Dizziness and falling in elderly psychiatric outpatients. *American Journal of Psychiatry*, 1980, *137*, 203-206.

Bockoven, J. S., & Solomon, J. C. Comparison of two five-year follow-up studies: 1947 to 1952 and 1967-1972. *American Journal of Psychiatry*, 1975, *132*, 796-801.

Borriello, J. F. Group psychotherapy with acting out patients: Specific problems and techniques. *American Journal of Psychotherapy*, 1979, *33*, 521–530.

Bowlby, J. The making and breaking of affectional bonds: II. Some principles of psychotherapy. *British Journal of Psychiatry*, 1977, *130*, 421–431.

Brandes, N. S. Adolescent therapy through the eyes of a group therapist. *Groups: A Journal of Group Dynamics and Psychotherapy*, 1977, *8*, 2–7.

Bratter, T. E. Responsible therapeutic eros: The psychotherapist who cares enough to define and enforce behavior limits with potentially suicidal adolescents. *Counseling Psychologist*, 1975, *5*, 97–104.

Brodsky, A. M. Countertransference issues and the woman therapist: Sex and the student therapist. *The Clinical Psychologist*, Winter 1977, pp. 12–14.

Broverman, I. K., Broverman, D. M., Clarkson, F. E., Rosenkrantz, P., & Vogel, S. R. Sex-role stereotypes and clinical judgments of mental health. *Journal of Consulting and Clinical Psychology*, 1970, *34*, 1–7.

Bruch, H. *Learning psychotherapy*. Cambridge, Mass.: Harvard University Press, 1974.

Buck, M. R. Peer counseling from a black perspective. *Journal of Black Psychology*, 1977, *3*, 107–113.

Buckley, P., Karasu, T. B., & Charles, E. Common mistakes in psychotherapy. *American Journal of Psychiatry*, 1979, *136*, 1578–1580.

Butcher, J. N., & Koss, M. P. Research on brief and crisis-oriented therapies. In S. L. Garfield & A. E. Bergin (Eds.), *Handbook of psychotherapy and behavior change* (2nd ed.) New York: Wiley, 1978.

Cameron, N. C. *Personality development and psychopathology: A dynamic approach*. Boston: Houghton Mifflin, 1963.

Carkhuff, R., & Berenson, B. *Beyond counseling and psychotherapy*. New York: Holt, Rinehart and Winston, 1967.

Carpenter, W. T., McGlashan, T. H., & Strauss, J. S. The treatment of acute schizophrenia without drugs: An investigation of some current assumptions. *American Journal of Psychiatry*, 1977, *134*, 14–20.

Carroll, C. F., & Reppucci, N. D. Meanings that professionals attach to labels for children. *Journal of Consulting and Clinical Psychology*, 1978, *46*, 372–374.

Carter, C. A. Advantages of being a woman therapist. *Psychotherapy: Theory, Research & Practice*, 1971, *8*, 297–300.

Carter, J. H. The black aged: A strategy for future mental health services. *Journal of the American Geriatrics Society*, 1978, *26*, 553–556.

Cavenar, J., & Harris, M. A. A "folie a deux" dystonic reaction. *American Journal of Psychiatry*, 1980, *137*, 99–100.

Chambers, C. A., & Naylor, G. J. A controlled trial of L-tryptophan in mania. *British Journal of Psychiatry*, 1978, *132*, 555–559.

Chappel, N. J., Jaffe, J. H., & Senay, E. C. A controlled study using cyclazocine in the treatment of narcotic addiction. *American Journal of Drug and Alcohol Abuse*, 1974, *1*, 233–242.

Chesler, P. *Women and madness*. New York: Doubleday, 1972.

Chouinard, G., & Jones, B. D. Neuroleptic-induced supersensitivity psychosis: Clinical and pharmacologic characteristics. *American Journal of Psychiatry*, 1980, *137*, 99–100.

Cohen, B. D. Effects of job interviewer knowledge of label on self-esteem of male ex-offenders and former mental patients (Doctoral dissertation, George Peabody College for Teachers, 1977). *Dissertation Abstracts International*, 1978, *38*, 3868B-3869B. (University Microfilms No. 7731613)

Cook, D. W., Kunce, J. J., & Getsenger, S. H. Perceptions of the disabled and counseling effectiveness. *Rehabilitation Counseling Bulletin*, 1976, *19*, 470–475.

Corey, G., Corey, M. S., & Callanan, P. *Professional and ethical issues in counseling and psychotherapy.* Monterey, Calif.: Brooks/Cole, 1979.

Corrigan, E. M. *Alcoholic women in treatment.* New York: Oxford University Press, 1980.

Cousins, N. *Anatomy of an illness as perceived by the patient.* New York: Norton, 1979.

Covert, A. B., Rodrigues, T., & Solomon, K. The use of mechanical and chemical restraints in nursing homes. *Journal of the American Geriatrics Society,* 1977, *25,* 85–89.

Crocetti, G., Spiro, H. R., & Siassi, I. Psychiatry and social class. In T. J. Cottle & P. Whitten (Eds.), *Psychotherapy: Current perspectives.* New York: New Viewpoints, 1980.

Croghan, L. M., & Frutiger, A. D. Contracting with children: A therapeutic tool. *Psychotherapy: Theory, Research & Practice,* 1977, *14,* 32–40.

Cummings, N. A. Turning bread into stones: Our modern antimiracle. *American Psychologist,* 1979, *34,* 1119–1129.

Curlee-Salisbury, J. Perspectives on Alcoholics Anonymous. In N. J. Estes & M. E. Heinemann (Eds.), *Alcoholism: Developments, consequences and interventions.* Saint Louis: Mosby, 1977.

Davis, G. R. Depression: Some updated thoughts. *Journal of the American Academy of Psychoanalysis,* 1976, *4,* 411–424.

Davis, M. S. Privacy considerations in Medicaid fraud investigations: The unwarranted paper chase. *The Clinical Psychologist,* Spring 1979, *32,* 19–20.

Deikman, A., & Whitaker, L. Humanizing a psychiatric ward: Changing from drugs to psychotherapy. *Psychotherapy: Theory, Research & Practice,* 1979, *16,* 204–214.

de la Torre, J. Brief encounters: General and technical psychoanalytic considerations. *Psychiatry,* 1978, *32,* 440–449.

Derner, G. F. Psychology—a health profession or a settled issue, so why the question? *The Clinical Psychologist,* Spring 1977, *30,* 3–6. (a)

Derner, G. F. Sexism, the Irish, the Protestant Ethnic, 1860 and whatever, but health is a problem in living. *The Clinical Psychologist,* Spring 1977, *30,* 7–8. (b)

Deutsch, C. B., & Kramer, N. Outpatient group psychotherapy for the elderly: An alternative to institutionalization. *Hospital and Community Psychiatry,* 1977, *28,* 440–442.

DiGiacomo, J. N., & Cornfield, R. Implications of increased dosages of neuroleptic medications during psychotherapy. *American Journal of Psychiatry,* 1979, *136,* 824–827.

Dingman, P. Personal communication, August 26, 1980.

Dinoff, M., Rickard, H. C., Love, W., & Elder, I. A patient writes his own report. *Adolescence,* 1978, *13,* 135–141.

Donahue, J. J., & Costar, J. W. Counselor discrimination against young women in career selection. *Journal of Counseling Psychology,* 1977, *24,* 481–486.

Donovan, H. H., & Mitchell, H. D., Jr. Preferences for older versus younger counselors among a group of elderly persons. *Journal of Counseling Psychology,* 1979, *26,* 514–518.

Dopson, C. Unresolved grief presenting as chronic lymphedema of the hand. *American Journal of Psychiatry,* 1979, *136,* 1333–1334.

Dubos, R. *Mirage of health.* New York: Harper and Brothers, 1959.

Ehrlich, R. P., D'Angelli, A. R., & Danish, S. J. Comparative effectiveness of six counselor verbal responses. *Journal of Counseling Psychology,* 1979, *26,* 390–398.

Eisenberg, L. Definitions of dyslexia: Their consequences for research and policy. In A. L. Benton & D. Pearl (Eds.), *Dyslexia: An appraisal of current knowledge.* New York: Oxford University Press, 1978.

Eisenbud, R. J. Countertransference issues in women therapists: Value conflicts between women therapists and woman patients. *The Clinical Psychologist,* Winter 1977, pp. 14–17.

Erikson, K. T. *In search of common ground: Conversations with Erik H. Erikson and Huey P. Newton.* New York: Norton, 1973.

Ersner-Hershfield, S., Abramowitz, S. I., & Baren, J. Incentive effects of choosing a therapist. *Journal of Clinical Psychology,* 1979, *35,* 404–406.

Evans, R., & diScipio, W. Nonpharmacologic factors in the administration of p.r.n. psychotropic medication on an adolescent unit. *American Journal of Psychiatry*, 1980, *137*, 123–124.

Everstine, L., Everstine, D. S., Heymann, G. M., True, R. H., Frey, D. H., Johnson, H. G. & Seiden, R. H. Privacy and confidentiality in psychotherapy. *American Psychologist*, 1980, *35*, 828–840.

Fauman, M. A. Tricyclic antidepressant prescription by general hospital physicians. *American Journal of Psychiatry*, 1980, *137*, 490–491.

Feldstein, J. C. Effects of counselor sex and sex role and client sex on clients' perceptions and self-disclosure in a counseling analogue study. *Journal of Counseling Psychology*, 1979, *26*, 437–443.

Felipe-Russo, N. Time to focus upon women: The Mental Health Systems Act. *Clinical Psychologist*, 1979, *33*, 18–19.

Fenichel, O. *The psychoanalytic theory of neurosis*. New York: Norton, 1945.

Fiedler, F. E. The concept of an ideal therapeutic relationship. *Journal of Consulting Psychology*, 1950, *14*, 436–445.

Fitzgerald, L. F., & Crites, J. O. Toward a career psychology of women: What do we know? What do we need to know? *Journal of Counseling Psychology*, 1980, *27*, 44–62.

Flexner, A. Is social work a profession? In *Proceedings of the National Conference of Charities and Corrections*. Baltimore: Social Work, 1915.

Foster, G., & Keech, V. Teacher reactions to the label of Educable Mentally Retarded. *Education and Training of the Mentally Retarded*, 1977, *12*, 307–311.

Frank, J. D. *Persuasion and healing: A comparative study of psychotherapy*. Baltimore: Johns Hopkins Press, 1973.

Fredericks, R. S., & Finkle, P. Schizophrenic performance on the Halsted-Reitan neuropsychological test battery. *Journal of Clinical Psychology*, 1978, *34*, 26–30.

Freud, S. [Fragment of an analysis of a case of hysteria. *The standard version of the complete psychological works* (Vol. 7).] London: Hogarth Press, 1953. (Originally published 1905.)

Frey, D. D., Hetherington, R. W., & Glassman, D. The use of prescription drugs in treatment of first-time psychiatric admissions to University Hospital, Saskatoon. *Social Science and Medicine*, 1978, *12*, 169–174.

Friedman, L. Defining psychotherapy. *Contemporary Psychoanalysis*, 1976, *12*, 258–269.

Fromm-Reichman, F. *Principles of intensive psychotherapy*. Chicago: University of Chicago Press, 1950.

Fry, P. S., Kropf, G., & Coe, K. J. Effects of counselor and client racial similarity on the counselor's response pattern and skills. *Journal of Counseling Psychology*, 1980, *27*, 130–137.

Fuller, C., & Kern, R. The effect of hostile clients on the opposite-race counselor. *Journal of Non-White Concerns in Personnel and Guidance*, 1978, *6*, 169–174.

Furgeri, L. B. The futility of child therapy. In T. J. Cottle & P. Whitten (Eds.), *Psychotherapy: Current perspectives*. New York: New Viewpoints, 1980.

Galanter, M. The "Relief Effect": A sociobiological model for neurotic distress and large-group therapy. *American Journal of Psychiatry*, 1978, *135*, 588–591.

Gale, M. S., Beck, S., & Springer, K. Effects of therapists' bias on diagnosis and disposition of emergency service patients. *Hospital and Community Psychiatry*, 1978, *29*, 705–708.

Gardos, G., & Cole, J. Maintenance antipsychotic therapy: Is the cure worse than the disease? *American Journal of Psychiatry*, 1976, *133*, 1237–1245.

Garmezy, N. DSM-III, never mind the psychologists: Is it good for the children? *The Clinical Psychologist*, Spring/Summer 1978, *31*, 1; 4–6

Garrison, J. E. Written vs. verbal preparation of patients for group psychotherapy. *Psychotherapy: Theory, Research and Practice*, 1978, *15*, 130–134.

Gay, R. L. The clinical psychologist and psychotropic medication. *The Clinical Psychologist*, Spring/Summer 1978, *3*, 1, 7.

Gelso, C. J. Gratification: A pivotal point in psychotherapy. *Psychotherapy: Theory, Research and Practice*, 1979, *16*, 276–281.

Gevinson, H. L. Termination of psychotherapy: Some salient issues. *Social Casework*, 1977, *58*, 480–489.

Gibbons, F. Y., Sawin, L. G., & Gibbons, B. N. Evaluations of mentally retarded persons: Sympathy or patronization? *American Journal of Mental Deficiency*, 1979, *84*, 124–131.

Giovacchini, P. L. The impact of delusion and the delusion of impact. *Contemporary Psychoanalysis*, 1977, *13*, 429–441.

Glasser, W. Promoting client strength through positive addiction. *Canadian Counsellor*, 1977, *11*, 173–175.

Glenn, M., & Kunnes, R. *Repression or revolution? Therapy in the United States today*. New York: Harper & Row, 1973.

Goldberg, C. Termination— A meaningful pseudodilemma in psychotherapy. *Psychotherapy: Theory, Research and Practice*, 1975, *12*, 341–343.

Goldberg, C. *Therapeutic partnership: Ethical concerns in psychotherapy*. New York: Springer, 1977.

Gottsegen, G. B., & Gottsegen, M. G. Countertransference: The professional identity defense. *Psychotherapy: Theory, Research and Practice*, 1979, *16*, 57–60.

Greer, J. G., & Davis, T. B. Drug treatment: Factors contributing to high risk in institutions. *Exceptional Children*, 1977, *43*, 451–453.

Griffith, M. S. The influences of race on the psychotherapeutic relationship. *Psychiatry*, 1977, *40*, 27–40.

Gross, M. The impact of ataractic drugs on a mental hospital outpatient clinic. *American Journal of Psychiatry*, 1960, *117*, 444–447.

Gunn, A. E. Mental impairment in the elderly: Medical-legal assessment. *Journal of the American Geriatrics Society*, 1977, *25*, 193–198.

Gurman, A. S., & Kniskern, D. P. Research on marital and family therapy: Progress, perspective, and prospect. In S. L. Garfield, & A. E. Bergin (Eds.), *Handbook of psychotherapy and behavior change* (2nd ed.) New York: Wiley, 1978.

Gynther, M. D., & Green, S. B. Accuracy may make a difference, but does a difference make for accuracy? A response to Pritchard and Rosenblatt. *Journal of Consulting and Clinical Psychology*, 1980, *48*, 268–272.

Haley, J. The art of being a failure as a therapist. *American Journal of Orthopsychiatry*, 1969, *39*, 691–695.

Hare-Mustin, R. T. Courage to look within: A discussant's view of countertransference. *The Clinical Psychologist*, Winter 1977, pp. 17, 22.

Hare-Mustin, R. T., Maracek, J., Kaplan, A. G., & Liss-Levinson, N. Rights of clients, responsibilities of therapists. *American Psychologist*, 1979; *34*, 3–16.

Hayes, M. The responsiveness of mentally retarded children to psychotherapy. *Smith College Studies in Social Work*, 1977, *47*, 112–153.

Hill, C. E., Tanney, M. F., & Leonard, M. M. Counselor reactions to female clients: Type of problem, age of client, and sex of counselor. *Journal of Counseling Psychology*, 1977, *24*, 60–65.

Hirsh, H. L. Will your medical records get you into trouble? *The Clinical Psychologist*, Spring 1979, *32*, 17–19.

Hoehn-Saric, R. Emotions and psychotherapies. *American Journal of Psychotherapy*, 1977, *31*, 83–96.

Holahan, C. J., & Slaikeu, K. A. Effects of contrasting degrees of privacy on client self-disclosure in a counseling setting. *Journal of Counseling Psychology*, 1977, *24*, 55–59.

Hollon, S. D., & Beck, A. T. Psychotherapy and drug therapy: Comparison and combinations. In S. L. Garfield & A. E. Bergin (Eds.), *Handbook of psychotherapy and behavior change* (2nd ed.). New York: Wiley, 1978.

Honigfeld, G., & Howard, A. *Psychiatric drugs: A desk reference* (2nd ed.) New York: Academic Press, 1978.

Hubble, M. A., & Gelso, C. J. Effect of counselor attire in an initial interview. *Journal of Counseling Psychology*, 1978, *25*, 581–584.

Ingebretsen, R. Psychotherapy with the elderly. *Psychotherapy: Theory, Research & Practice*, 1977, *14*, 319–332.

Ivey, A. E., & Simek-Downing, L. *Counseling and psychotherapy.* Englewood Cliffs, N.J.: Prentice Hall, 1980.

Jacobs, D. F. Standards for psychologists. In H. Dorken & Associates (Eds.), *The professional psychologist today.* San Francisco: Jossey-Bass, 1976.

Jacobs, D., Charles, E., Jacobs, T., Weinstein, H., & Mann, D. Preparation for treatment of the disadvantaged patient: Effects on disposition and outcome. *American Journal of Orthopsychiatry*, 1972, *42*, 666–674.

Jones, A., & Seagull, A. A. Dimensions of the relationship between the black client and the white therapist. *American Psychologist*, 1977, *32*, 850–855.

Jourard, S. M. *Disclosing man to himself.* Princeton, N.J.: Van Nostrand, 1968.

Jourard, S. M. *The transparent self.* New York: Van Nostrand, 1971.

June, L. E. A comparison of self-limited, externally limited and unlimited counseling and psychotherapy. *Psychotherapy: Theory, Research and Practice*, 1979, *16*, 39–45.

Kamin, I., & Coughlin, J. Subjective experiences of outpatient psychotherapy. *American Journal of Psychotherapy*, 1963, *17*, 660.

Karenza, M. R. Chinese psychosocial therapy: A strategic model for mental health. *Psychotherapy: Theory, Research and Practice*, 1978, *15*, 101–107.

Karon, B. P., & Vanden Bos, G. R. The consequences of psychotherapy for schizophrenics. *Psychotherapy: Theory, Research & Practice*, 1972, *9*, 111–119.

Karon, B. P., & Vanden Bos, G. R. Issues in current research on psychotherapy vs. medication in treatment of schizophrenics. *Psychotherapy: Theory, Research & Practice*, 1975, *12*, 143–148. (a)

Karon, B. P., & Vanden Bos, G. R. Psychotherapy works . . . and costs less too: Clinical outcome and treatment costs of psychotherapy versus medication for schizophrenics. Paper presented at the meeting of the American Psychological Association, Chicago, 1975. (b)

Kastenbaum, R. Personality theory, therapeutic approaches, and the elderly client. In M. A. Storandt, I. C. Siegler, & M. F. Elias (Eds.), *The clinical psychology of aging.* New York: Plenum, 1978.

Kazdin, A. E. The application of operant techniques in treatment, rehabilitation, and education. In S. L. Garfield & A. E. Bergin (Eds.), *Handbook of psychotherapy and behavior change* (2nd ed.) New York: Wiley, 1978.

Keilson, M. V., Dworkin, F. H., & Gelso, C. J. The effectiveness of time-limited psychotherapy in a university counseling center. *Journal of Clinical Psychology*, 1979, *35*, 631–636.

Kemp, C. G. *Intangibles in counseling.* New York: Houghton Mifflin, 1967.

Kepics, J. G. Tracking errors in psychotherapy. *American Journal of Psychotherapy*, 1979, *33*, 365–377.

Kinney, J., & Leaton, G. *Loosening the grip: A handbook of alcohol information.* St. Louis: Moseby, 1978.

Kirsch, I. Teaching clients to be their own therapists: A case-study illustration. *Psychotherapy: Theory, Research and Practice*, 1978, *15*, 302–305.

Korchin, S. J. Clinical psychology and minority problems. *American Psychologist*, 1980, *35*, 262–269.

Koss, M. P. Length of psychotherapy for clients seen in private practice. *Journal of Consulting and Clinical Psychology*, 1979, *47*, 210–212.

Kronsky, B. J. Feminism in psychotherapy. *Journal of Contemporary Psychotherapy*, 1971, *3*, 89–98.

Kupst, M. J., & Schulman, J. L. Comparing professional and lay expectations of psychotherapy. *Psychotherapy: Theory, Research and Practice*, 1979, *16*, 237–243.

Kwawer, J. Transference and countertransference in homosexuality: Changing psychoanalytic views. *American Journal of Psychotherapy*, 1980, *34*, 72–80.

Lager, G., & Zwerling, I. Time orientation and psychotherapy in the ghetto. *American Journal of Psychiatry*, 1980, *137*, 306–309.

Lane, P. J. & Spruill, J. To tell or not to tell: The psychotherapist's dilemma. *Psychotherapy: Theory, Research and Practice*, 1980, *17*, 202–209.

Leff, J. P., & Wing, J. K. Trial maintenance therapy in schizophrenia. *British Medical Journal*, 1971, *116*, 559–604.

Lerman, H. Some thoughts on cross-gender psychotherapy. *Psychotherapy: Theory, Research & Practice*, 1978, *15*, 248–250.

Levine, H. D., & Sice, J. Effects of set, setting and sedatives on reaction time. *Perceptual and Motor Skills*, 1976, *42*, 403–412.

London, P. *The modes and morals of psychotherapy*. New York: Holt, Rinehart and Winston, 1964.

Loney, J. Hyperkinesis comes of age: What do we know and where should we go? *American Journal of Orthopsychiatry*, 1980, *50*, 28–42.

Longwell, B., Miller, J., & Nichols, A. W. Counselor effectiveness in a methadone maintenance program. *International Journal of the Addictions*, 1978, *13*, 307–315.

Lonowski, D. J., Seterling, F. E., & Kennedy, J. C. Gradual reduction of neuroleptic drugs among chronic schizophrenics. *Acta Psychiatrica Scandinavica*, 1978, *52*, 99–102.

Lowery, C. R., & Higgins, R. L. Analogue investigation of the relationship between clients' sex and treatment recommendations. *Journal of Consulting and Clinical Psychology*, 1979, *47*, 792–794.

Mahoney, M. J., & Arnkoff, D. B. Cognitive and self-control therapies. In S. L. Garfield & A. E. Bergin (Eds.), *Handbook of psychotherapy and behavior change* (2nd ed.) New York: Wiley, 1978.

Maier, H. W. *Three theories of child development*. New York: Harper & Row, 1978.

Malett, S. D., Spokane, A. R., & Vance, F. L. Effects of vocationally relevant information on the expressed and measured interests of freshman males. *Journal of Counseling Psychology*, 1978, *25*, 292–298.

Mann, J. N. *Time-limited psychotherapy*. Cambridge, Mass.: Harvard University Press, 1973.

Manos, M., Taratsidis, I., Pappas, K., & Routsonis, C. Maintenance antipsychotic pharmacotherapy relapse and length of stay out of the hospital in chronic schizophrenics in Greece. *Journal of Nervous and Mental Disease*, 1977, *165*, 361–363.

Marmor, J. Short-term dynamic psychotherapy. *American Journal of Psychiatry*, 1979, *136*, 149–155.

May, P. R. A. *Treatment of schizophrenia: A comparative study of five treatment methods*. New York: Science House, 1968.

Mayer, D. Y. Psychotropic drugs and the anti-depressed personality. *British Journal of Medical Psychology*, 1975, *48*, 349–357.

Mayo, J. A., O'Connell, R. A., & O'Brian, J. D. Families of manic-depressive patients: Effect of treatment. *American Journal of Psychiatry*, 1979, *136*, 1535–1539.

McGhee, P. E. *Humor: Its origin and development*. San Francisco: W. H. Freeman and Company, 1979.

McGill, J. C. MMPI score differences among Anglo, Black, and Mexican-American welfare recipients. *Journal of Clinical Psychology*, 1980, *36*, 147–151.

McKitrick, D. S., & Gelso, C. J. Initial client expectancies in time-limited counseling. *Journal of Counseling Psychology*, 1978, *25*, 246–249.

McLean, P. D., & Hakstian, A. R. Clinical depression: Comparative efficacy of outpatient treatments. *Journal of Consulting and Clinical Psychology*, 1979, *47*, 818–836.

Meares, R. The secret. In T. J. Cottle & P. Whitten (Eds.), *Psychotherapy: Current perspectives*. New York: New Viewpoints, 1980.

Medical Economics Company. *Physician's desk reference* (34th ed.). Oradell, N. J.: Author, 1981.

Menninger, K. *A manual for psychiatric case study*. New York: Grune and Stratton, 1960.

Merluzzi, B. H., & Merluzzi, T. V. Influence of client race on counselors' assessment of case materials. *Journal of Counseling Psychology*, 1978, *25*, 399–404.

Meyer, R. G., & Smith, S. R. A crisis in group psychotherapy. *American Psychologist*, 1977, *32*, 638–643.

Michels, R. Professional ethics and social values. In T. J. Cottle & P. Whitten (Eds.), *Psychotherapy: Current perspectives*. New York: New Viewpoints, 1980.

Mintz, I. A note on the addictive personality: Addiction to placebos. *American Journal of Psychiatry*, 1977, *134*, 327.

Mitchell, J. E., & Gillum, R. Weight-dependent arrhythmia in a patient with anorexia nervosa. *American Journal of Psychiatry*, 1980, *137*, 377–378.

Montague, A. *Anthropology and human nature*. Boston: Expanding Horizons, 1957.

Morrison, J. K. A consumer-oriented approach to psychotherapy. *Psychotherapy: Theory, Research, and Practice*, 1979, *16*, 381–384.

Morrison, J. K. A consumer approach. *American Psychologist*. 1980, *35*, 111–112.

Murray, E. J., & Jacobson, C. I. Cognition and learning in traditional and behavioral therapy. In S. L. Garfield & A. E. Bergin (Eds.), *Handbook of psychotherapy and behavior change* (2nd ed.) New York: Wiley, 1978.

Nair, N. P. Drug therapy of schizophrenia in the community. *Journal of Orthomolecular Psychiatry*, 1977, *6*, 348–353.

Nash, J. L., & Cavenar, J. O. Free psychotherapy: An inquiry into resistance. *American Journal of Psychiatry*, 1976, *133*, 1066–1069.

Nelson, W. M., & Groman, W. D. Temporal perspective from the Gestalt therapy assumption of present centeredness. *Psychotherapy: Theory, Research and Practice*, 1978, *15*, 277–284.

Norton, C. A. Effects of training in detection and use of non-verbal behavior on counselor effectiveness (Doctoral dissertation, University of Northern Colorado, 1978). *Dissertation Abstracts International*, 1978, *38*, 5582B. (University Microfilms No. 7805513.)

Olin, H. S. Psychotherapy of the chronically suicidal patient. *American Journal of Psychotherapy*, 1976, *30*, 570–575.

Oliver, L. Principles drafted for therapy and counseling with women. *APA Monitor*, December 1978, p. 11.

Olson, E. J., Bank, L., & Jarvik, L. F. Gerovital-H$_3$: A clinical trial as an antidepressant. *Journal of Gerontology*, 1978, *33*, 514–520.

Orlinsky, D. E., & Howard, K. I. The relation of process to outcome in psychotherapy. In S. L. Garfield & A. E. Bergin (Eds.), *Handbook of psychotherapy and behavior change* (2nd ed.) New York: Wiley, 1978.

Otteson, J. P. Curative caring: The use of buddy groups with chronic schizophrenics. *Journal of Consulting and Clinical Psychology*, 1979, *47*, 649–651.

Padow, E. The experiencing of will: Turning points in therapy. *Journal of the Otto Rank Association*, 1977–1978, *12*, 54–58.

Parloff, M. B., Waskow, I. E., & Wolfe, B. E. Research on therapist variables in relation to process and outcome. In S. L. Garfield & A. E. Bergin (Eds.), *Handbook of psychotherapy and behavior change* (2nd ed.) New York: Wiley, 1978.

Pasamanick, B., Scarpitti, S. R., & Lefton, M. Phenothiazines in prevention of psychiatric hospitalization. IV. Delay or prevention of hospitalization, a re-evaluation. *Archives of General Psychiatry*, 1967, *16*, 98–101.

Pasternack, S. A. The psychotherapy fee: An issue in residency training. *Diseases of the Nervous System*, 1977, *38*, 913–916.

Patterson, C. H. New approaches in counseling: Healthy diversity or anti-therapeutic? In T. J. Cottle & P. Whitten (Eds.), *Psychotherapy: Current perspectives*. New York: New Viewpoints, 1980.

Paul, O. H. Psychotherapy as a unique and unambiguous event. *Contemporary Psychoanalysis*, 1976, *12*, 21–57.

Pepitone-Rockwell, F. Patterns of rape and approaches to care. *The Journal of Family Practice*, 1978, *6*, 521–529.

Peterson, D. R. Is psychology a profession? *American Psychologist*, 1976, *31*, 553–560.

Phillips, D. R., & Grover, G. A. Assertive training with children. *Psychotherapy: Theory, Research & Practice*, 1979, *16*, 171–177.

Plotkin, R. Confidentiality in group counseling. *APA Monitor*, March 1978, 14.

Plotkin, R. The view from the courts. *APA Monitor*, January 1980, *11*, 12.

Pritchard, D. A., & Rosenblatt, A. Racial bias in the MMPI: A methodological review. *Journal of Consulting and Clinical Psychology*, 1980, *48*, 263–267.

Rice, I. K., & Rice, D. E. Implications of the women's liberation movement for psychotherapy. *American Journal of Psychiatry*, 1973, *130*, 191–196.

Rickels, K., Case, W. G., Csanalosi, I., Pereira, J. A., Sandler, K. R., & Schless, A. P. Loxipane in neurotic anxiety: A controlled trial. *Current Therapeutic Research*, 1978, *23*, 111–120.

Riscalla, L. M. Professional child abuse: How children are abused while being helped. *Journal of Clinical Child Psychology*, 1980, *9*, 72–73.

Roach, J. L., & Maizler, J. S. Individual psychotherapy with the institutionalized aged. *American Journal of Orthopsychiatry*, 1977, *47*, 275–283.

Rogers, C. R. *Counseling and psychotherapy*. Boston: Houghton Mifflin, 1942.

Rogers, C. R. *On becoming a person*. Boston: Houghton Mifflin, 1961.

Rogers, C. *Carl Rogers on encounter groups*. New York: Harper & Row, 1970.

Roll, S., Miller, L., & Martinez, R. Common errors in psychotherapy with Chicanos. *Psychotherapy: Theory, Research and Practice*, 1980, *17*, 158–168.

Rosenthal, R. *Experimenter effects in behavioral research*. New York: Appleton-Century-Crofts, 1966.

Ross, A. O. *Psychological disorders of children*. New York: McGraw-Hill, 1974.

Ross, A. O. *Psychological disorders of children: A behavioral approach to theory, research and therapy* (2nd ed.) New York: McGraw-Hill, 1980.

Roth, L. H. & Meisel, A. Dangerousness, confidentiality, and the duty to warn. *American Journal of Psychiatry*, 1977, *134*, 508–511.

Ruesch, J. Communication difficulties among psychiatrists. *American Journal of Psychotherapy*, 1956, *10*, 432–447.

Ruesch, J. *Therapeutic communication*. New York: Norton, 1973.

Rutter, M. Prevalence and types of dyslexia. In A. E. Benton & D. Pearl (Eds.). *Dyslexia: An appraisal of current knowledge*. New York: Oxford University Press, 1978.

Ryle, A. The focus in brief, interpretive psychotherapy: Dilemmas, traps, and snags as target problems. *British Journal of Psychiatry*, 1979, *134*, 46–54.

Rynearson, R. R. Touching people. *Journal of Clinical Psychiatry*, 1978, *39*, 492.

Santos, A. B., & McCurdy, L. Delirium after abrupt withdrawal from doxepin: Case report. *American Journal of Psychiatry*, 1980, *137*, 239–240.

Saretsky, L. Sex related countertransference: Issues of a female therapist. *Clinical Psychologist*, Winter 1977, pp. 1, 10.

Schacht, T., & Nathan, P. E. But is it good for the psychologists? Appraisal and status of DSM-III. *American Psychologist*, 1977, *32*, 1017–1025.

Schaffer, K. F. *Sex-role issues in mental health*. Reading, Mass.: Addison-Wesley, 1980.

Schain, R. J. *Neurology of childhood learning disorders* (2nd ed.) Baltimore: Williams & Wilkins, 1977.

Scheff, T. J. (Ed.) *Labeling madness.* Englewood Cliffs, N. J.: Prentice-Hall, 1975.

Schimel, J. L. Some thoughts on the uses of wit and humor in the treatment of adolescents. *New Directions for Mental Health Services*, 1980, *5*, 15-23.

Schmidt, J. P., & Hancey, R. Social class and psychiatric treatment: Application of a decision-making model to use patterns in a cost-free clinic. *Journal of Consulting and Clinical Psychology*, 1979, *47*, 771-772.

Schofield, W. *Psychotherapy: The purchase of friendship.* Englewood Cliffs, N.J.: Prentice-Hall, 1964.

Shah, S. Privileged communications, confidentiality, and privacy. *Professional Psychology*, 1969, *1*, 56-69.

Shapiro, A. K., & Morris, L. A. The placebo effect in medical and psychological therapies. In S. L. Garfield & A. E. Bergin (Eds.), *Handbook of psychotherapy and behavior change* (2nd ed.) New York: Wiley, 1978.

Shertzer, B., & Stone, S. C. *Fundamentals of counseling* (3rd ed.) Boston: Houghton Mifflin, 1980.

Sidel, R. Mental diseases in China and their treatment. In T. J. Scheff (Ed.), *Labeling madness.* Englewood Cliffs, N. J.: Prentice-Hall, 1975.

Siegel, M. Confidentiality. *The Clinical Psychologist*, Fall 1976, *30*, 1:23.

Siegel, M. More on confidentiality. *The Clinical Psychologist*, Spring 1979, *32*, 17.

Sloane, R. B., Staples, F. R., Cristol, A. H., Yorkston, N. J., & Whipple, K. *Psychotherapy versus behavior therapy.* Cambridge, Mass.: Harvard University Press, 1975.

Slovenko, R. On confidentiality. *Contemporary Psychoanalysis*, 1976, *12*, 109-139.

Slovenko, R. Group psychotherapy: Privileged communication and confidentiality. *Journal of Psychiatry and the Law*, 1977, *5*, 405-466.

Smith, M. L. Sex bias in counseling and psychotherapy. *Psychological Bulletin*, 1980, *87*, 392-407.

Smyer, M. A., & Gatz, M. Aging and mental health: Business as usual? *American Psychologist*, 1979, *34*, 240-246.

Sobel, D. Placebo Studies are not just "all in your mind." *The New York Times*, January 6, 1980, 129, E9.

Spensley, J., & Blacker, K. H. Countertransference and other feelings in the psychotherapist. *Diseases of the Nervous System*, 1977, *38*, 595-598.

Spiegel, S. B. Separate principles for counselors of women: A new form of sexism. *Counseling Psychologist*, 1979, *8*, 49-50.

Standal, S. W., & Corsini, R. *Critical incidents in psychotherapy.* Englewood Cliffs, N.J.: Prentice-Hall, 1959.

Stein, L. S. Self-help for therapists: The advantages of drug treatment. *Psychotherapy: Theory, Research & Practice*, 1975, *12*, 314-316.

Steiner, G. L. A survey to identify factors in therapists' selection of a therapeutic orientation. *Psychotherapy: Theory, Research & Practice*, 1978, *15*, 371-374.

Steinzor, B. *The healing partnership: The patient as colleague in psychotherapy.* New York: Harper and Row, 1967.

Stokes, J., Fuehrer, A., & Childs, L. Gender differences in self-disclosure to various target persons. *Journal of Counseling Psychology*, 1980, *27*, 192-198.

Storandt, M. Other approaches to therapy. In M. A. Storandt, I. C. Siegler, & M. F. Elias (Eds.), *The clinical psychology of aging.* New York: Plenum, 1978.

Strassberg, G. S., Anchor, K. N., Cunningham, J., & Elkins, D. Successful outcome and number of sessions: When do counselors think enough is enough? *Journal of Counseling Psychology*, 1977, *24*, 477-480.

Strauss, J. S., Downey, T. W., & Ware, S. Treating children and adolescents in the same psychiatric inpatient setting. *American Journal of Orthopsychiatry*, 1980, *50*, 165-168.

Strupp, H. A reformulation of the dynamics of the therapist's contribution. In A. S. Gurnan & A. M. Razin (Eds.), *Effective psychotherapy: A handbook of research*. New York: Pergamon, 1977.

Strupp, H. H. Psychotherapy research and practice: An overview. In S. L. Garfield & A. E. Bergin (Eds.), *Handbook of psychotherapy and behavior change* (2nd ed.) New York: Wiley, 1978. (a)

Strupp, H. The therapist's theoretical orientation: An overrated variable. *Psychotherapy: Theory, Research and Practice*, 1978, *15*, 314-317. (b)

Strupp, H. A psychodynamicist looks at modern behavior therapy. *Psychotherapy: Theory, Research and Practice*, 1979, *16*, 124-131.

Sue, D. W., & Sue, D. Barriers to effective cross-cultural counseling. *Journal of Counseling Psychology*, 1977, *24*, 420-429.

Sviland, M. A. P. Helping elderly couples become sexually liberated: Psychosocial issues. In J. LoPiccolo & L. LoPiccolo (Eds.), *Handbook of sex therapy*. New York: Plenum, 1978.

Szasz, T. S. *The ethics of psychoanalysis*. New York: Basic Books, 1965.

Szasz, T. S. *The myth of mental illness*. New York: Harper & Row, 1961.

Tanney, M. F., & Birk, J. M. Women counselors for women clients? A review of the research. *The Counseling Psychologist*, 1976, *6*, 28-32.

Thorne, F. T. Eclectic psychotherapy. In R. Corsini (Ed.), *Current psychotherapies*. Itasca, Ill.: F. E. Peacock, 1973.

Tolbert, E. L. *An introduction to guidance*. Boston: Little, Brown, 1978.

Toomer, J. E. Males in psychotherapy. *The Counseling Psychologist*, 1978, *7*, 22-25.

Totman, R. Cognitive dissonance in the placebo treatment of insomnia: A pilot experiment. *British Journal of Medical Psychology*, 1976, *49*, 393-400.

Touliatos, J., & Lindholm, B. W. Psychopathology of Anglo and Chicano children. *Journal of Clinical Child Psychology*, 1980, *9*, 55-56.

Tuma, A. H., & May, P. R. A. Psychotherapy, drugs and therapist experience in the treatment of schizophrenia: A critique of the Michigan state project. *Psychotherapy: Theory, Research & Practice*, 1974, *12*, 138-142.

Van Hoose, W., & Kottler, J. A. *Ethical and legal issues in counseling and psychotherapy*. San Francisco: Jossey-Bass, 1977.

Wachtel, P. L. *Psychoanalysis and behavior therapy: Toward an integration*. New York: Basic Books, 1977.

Wachtel, P. L. What should we say to our patients?: On the wording of therapists' comments. *Psychotherapy: Theory, Research and Practice*, 1980, *17*, 183-188.

Wallick, M. M. Desensitization therapy with a fearful two year old. *American Journal of Psychiatry*, 1979, *136*, 1325-1326.

Wang, R. I., & Stockdale, S. L. A subjective and objective method assessing the efficacy of hypnotic medications in insomniacs. *Journal of Clinical Pharmacology*, 1977, *17*, 728-733.

Warren, L. W. The therapeutic status of consciousness-raising groups. *Professional Psychology*, 1976, *7*, 132-140.

Waxler, N. E. Is mental illness cured in traditional societies? *Culture, Medicine and Psychiatry*, 1977, *1*, 233-253.

Weinberg, J. R. Counseling the person with alcohol problems. In N. J. Estes & M. E. Heinemann (Eds.), *Alcoholism: Development, consequences, and intervention*. Saint Louis: Moseby, 1977.

Weintraub, W., & Aronson, J. A survey of patients in classical psychoanalysis: Some vital statistics. *Journal of Nervous and Mental Disease*, 1968, *146*, 98-102.

Wenegrat, A. Linguistic variables of therapist speech and accurate empathy ratings. *Psy-*

chotherapy: Theory, Research and Practice, 1976, *13*, 30–33.

Werry, J. S. Organic factors in childhood psychopathology. In H. C. Quay & J. S. Werry (Eds.), *Psychopathological disorders of childhood*. New York: Wiley, 1972.

Wilcox, E. Check mark. *Report of the Institute of Certified Public Accountants*. Ontario, Canada, 1964.

Wilder, D. H., Hoyt, A. E., Zettle, R. D., & Hauck, W. E. Client personality and preferred sex of counselor. *Psychotherapy: Theory, Research & Practice*, 1978, *15*, 135–139.

Wohl, J. Third parties and individual psychotherapy. *American Journal of Psychotherapy*, 1974, *28*, 527–547.

Wohlford, P. Clinical child psychology: The emerging specialty. *Clinical Psychologist*, 1979, *33*, 25–29.

Wollersheim, M. P., McFall, M., Hamilton, S. B., Hickey, C. S., & Bordewick, M. L. Effects of treatment rationale and problem severity on perceptions of psychological problems and counseling approaches. *Journal of Counseling Psychology*, 1980, *27*, 225–231.

Yalom, I. *The theory and practice of group psychotherapy* (2nd ed.) New York: Basic Book, 1975.

Zaro, J. S., Barach, R., Nedelman, P. J. & Dreiblatt, I. S. *A guide for beginning psychotherapists*. Cambridge, England: Cambridge University Press, 1978.

Author Index

Abramowitz, S. I., 41, 107
Adams, H., 8, 105
Adams, S., 25, 105
Ahn Toupin, E. S., 53, 105
Alagna, F. J., 5, 105
Albee, G. W., 99, 105
Albin, R., 10, 105
Allport, G. W., 44, 105
Allyon, T., 72, 105
American Psychiatric Association, 26, 27, 32, 36, 105
Anchor, K. N., 10, 114
Anderson, J. G., 37, 105
Andrade, E. H., 28, 105
Applebaum, S. A., 33, 105
Armstrong, H. E. Jr., 36, 105
Arnkoff, D. B., 12, 111
Aronson, J., 46, 115

Bank, L., 60, 112
Barach, R., 98, 116
Baren, J., 41, 107
Beck, A. T., 69, 109
Beck, S., 53, 108
Beier, E. G., 7, 105
Berenson, B., 27, 106
Bergman, H., 68, 69, 105
Berman, J., 51, 105
Berne, E., 37, 105
Birk, J. M., 50, 115
Blacker, K. H., 4, 10, 114
Blazer, D., 45, 105
Bloch, D., 35, 45, 105
Blumenthal, M. D., 69, 105

Bockoven, J. S., 70, 105
Booth, C., 36, 105
Bordewick, M. L., 24, 116
Borg, S., 68, 105
Borriello, J. F., 25, 106
Bowlby, J., 3, 106
Brandes, N. S., 37, 106
Bratter, T. E., 5, 106
Brodsky, A. M., 52, 106
Broverman, D. M., 51, 106
Broverman, I. K., 51, 106
Bruch, H., 2, 3, 7, 9, 16, 17, 22, 25, 27, 37, 45, 46, 106
Buck, M. R., 53, 106
Buckley, P., 22, 106
Butcher, J. N., 10, 106

Callanan, P., 11, 21, 36, 107
Cameron, N. C., 35, 49, 106
Carkhuff, R., 8, 27, 106
Carpenter, W. T., 65, 106
Carroll, C. F., 32, 106
Carter, C. A., 50, 106
Carter, J. H., 53, 106
Case, W. G., 60, 113
Cavenar, J., 23, 69, 106, 112
Chambers, C. A., 60, 106
Chappel, N. J., 60, 106
Charles, E., 22, 54, 106, 110
Chesler, P., 50, 106
Childs, L., 51, 114
Chouinard, G., 68, 106
Clarkson, F. E., 51, 106
Coe, K. J., 53, 54, 108

Cohen, B. D., 32, 106
Cole, J., 71, 108
Cook, D. W., 43, 106
Corey, G., 11, 21, 36, 107
Corey, M. S., 11, 21, 36, 107
Cornfield, R., 62, 107
Corrigan, E. M., 43, 50, 107
Corsini, R., 27, 48, 99, 114
Costar, J. W., 50, 107
Coughlin, J., 20, 110
Cousins, N., ix, 9, 19, 21, 30, 56, 61, 89, 107
Covert, A. B., 66, 107
Cowper, W., 26
Cristol, A. H., 12, 114
Crites, J. O., 50, 108
Crocetti, G., 33, 107
Croghan, L. M., 46, 107
Csanalosi, I., 60, 113
Cummings, N. A., 11, 19, 21, 73, 107
Cunningham, J., 10, 114
Curlee-Salisbury, J., 43, 107

D'Angelli, A. R., 4, 107
Danish, S. J., 4, 107
Davie, J. W., 69, 105
Davis, G. R., 32, 107
Davis, M. S., 97, 107
Davis, T. B., 71, 109
Deikman, A., 11, 72, 107
de la Torre, J., 10, 107
Derner, G. F., 99, 107
Deutsch, C. B., 46, 107
DiGiacomo, J. N., 62, 107
Dingman, P., 35, 107
Dinoff, M., 36, 107
di Scipio, W., 73, 108
Donahue, J. J., 50, 107
Donovan, H. H., 10, 107
Dopson, C., 66, 67, 107
Downey, T. W., 47, 115
Dreiblatt, I. S., 98, 116
Dubos, R., 34, 61, 107
Dworkin, F. H., 10, 110

Ehrlich, R. P., 4, 107
Eisenberg, L., 33, 107

Eisenbud, R. J., 52, 107
Erikson, K. T., 37, 107
Elder, I., 36, 107
Elkins, D., 10, 114
Ersner-Hershfield, S., 41, 107
Euripides, 14
Evans, R., 73, 108
Everstine, D. S., 90, 108
Everstine, L., 90, 91, 93, 95, 108

Fauman, M. A., 71, 108
Feldstein, J. C., 51, 108
Felipe-Russo, N., 50, 108
Fenichel, O., 8, 45, 46, 108
Fiedler, F. E., 11, 12, 108
Finkle, P., 60, 108
Fisher, J. D., 5, 105
Fitzgerald, L. F., 50, 108
Flexner, A., 17, 108
Foster, G., 32, 108
Frank, J. D., 21, 108
Fredricks, R. S., 60, 108
Freud, S., 8, 27, 99, 108
Frey, D. D., 50, 108
Frey, D. H., 90, 108
Friedman, L., 9, 108
Fromm-Reichman, F., 22, 108
Frutiger, A. D., 46, 107
Fry, P. S., 53, 54, 108
Fuehrer, A., 51, 114
Fuller, C., 53, 54, 108
Furgeri, L. B., 25, 108

Galanter, M., 37, 108
Gale, M. S., 53, 108
Gardos, G., 71, 108
Garmezy, N., 34, 108
Garrison, J. G., 24, 108
Gatz, M., 47, 114
Gay, J., 1
Gay, R. L., 71, 109
Gelso, C. J., 10, 17, 20, 21, 109, 110, 111
Getsenger, S. H., 43, 106
Gevinson, H. L., 10, 109
Gibbons, B. N., 32, 109
Gibbons, F. Y., 32, 109

Gillum, R., 68, 112
Giovacchini, P. L., 43, 45, 109
Glasser, W., 35, 109
Glassman, D., 50, 108
Glenn, M., 50, 109
Goldberg, C., 9, 10, 24, 109
Gottsegen, G. B., 12, 109
Gottsegen, M. G., 12, 109
Green, S. B., 53, 109
Greer, J. G., 71, 109
Griffith, M. S., 54, 109
Groman, W. D., 8, 112
Gross, M., 60, 109
Grover, G. A., 46, 113
Gunn, A. E., 47, 109
Gurman, A. S., 7, 10, 109
Gynther, M. D., 53, 109

Hakstian, A. R., 72, 112
Haley, J., 1, 109
Hamilton, S. B., 24, 116
Hancey, R., 53, 114
Hare-Mustin, R. T., 25, 52, 109
Harris, M. A., 69, 106
Hauck, W. E., 52, 116
Hayes, M., 43, 109
Hetherington, R. W., 50, 108
Heyman, G. M., 90, 108
Hickey, C. S., 24, 116
Higgins, R. L., 50, 111
Hill, C. E., 51, 109
Hirsch, H. L., 97, 109
Hoen-Saric, R., 12, 109
Holahan, C. J., 18, 109
Hollon, S. D., 69, 109
Holm, L., 68, 105
Honigfeld, G., 58, 59, 64, 67–69, 110
Howard, A., 58, 59, 64, 67–69, 110
Howard, K. I., 7, 112
Hoyt, A. E., 52, 116
Hubble, M. A., 18, 110

Ingebretsen, R., 46, 48, 110
Ivey, A. E., 10, 110

Jacobs, D., 17, 54, 110
Jacobs, T., 54, 110

Jacobson, C. I., 11, 19, 112
Jaffe, J. H., 60, 106
James, W., 26
Jarvik, L. F., 60, 112
Jefferys, C., 75
Johnson, H. G., 90, 108
Jones, A., 53, 110
Jones, B. D., 68, 106
Jourard, S. M., 7, 9, 11, 12, 16, 52, 73, 74, 89, 110
June, L. E., 10, 110

Kamin, I., 20, 110
Kandel, H. J., 72, 105
Kaplan, 25, 109
Karasu, T. B., 22, 106
Karenza, M. R., 37, 110
Karon, B. P., 11, 71, 72, 110
Kastenbaum, R., 47, 48, 110
Kazdin, A., 72, 110
Keech, V., 32, 108
Keilson, M. V., 10, 110
Kemp, C. G., 7, 110
Kennedy, J. C., 70, 111
Kepics, J. G., 3, 110
Kern, R., 53, 54, 108
Kinney, J., 17, 110
Kirsch, I., 36, 110
Kniskern, D. P., 7, 10, 109
Korchin, S. J., 53, 110
Koss, M. P., 10, 21, 106, 110
Kottler, J. A., 14, 115
Kramer, N., 46, 107
Kronsky, B. J., 50, 111
Kropf, G., 53, 54, 108
Kunce, J. J., 43, 106
Kunnes, R., 50, 109
Kupst, M. J., 19, 20, 111
Kwawer, J., 50, 111

Lager, G., 53, 111
Lane, P. J., 94, 111
Layman, D., 72, 105
Leaton, G., 17, 110
Leff, J. P., 60, 111
Lefton, M., 60, 112
Leonard, M. M., 51, 109

Lerman, H., 39, 111
Levine, H. D., 73, 111
Lindholm, B. W., 54, 115
Liss-Levinson, N., 25, 109
London, P., 17, 111
Loney, J., 71, 111
Longwell, B., 43, 111
Lonowski, D. J., 70, 111
Love, W., 36, 107
Lowery, C. R., 50, 111

Mahoney, M. J., 12, 111
Maier, H. W., 7, 9, 27, 37, 45, 46, 111
Maizler, J. S., 47, 113
Malett, S.D., 4, 111
Mann, D., 54, 111
Mann, J. N., 10, 111
Manos, M., 70, 111
Maracek, J., 25, 109
Marmor, J., 10, 111
Martinez, R., 32, 113
May, P. R. A., 72, 111, 115
Mayer, D. Y., 66, 111
Mayo, J. A., 66, 111
McCurdy, L., 69, 113
McFall, M., 24, 116
McGhee, P. E., 11, 111
McGill, J. C., 54, 111
McGlashen, T. H., 65, 106
McKitrick, D. S., 21, 111
McLean, P. D., 72, 112
Meares, R., 89, 112
Medical Economics Company, 59, 112
Meisel, A., 96, 113
Menninger, K., 93, 112
Merluzzi, B. H., 54, 112
Merluzzi, T. V., 54, 112
Meyer, R. G., 101, 112
Michels, R., 17, 18, 112
Miller, J., 43, 111
Miller, L., 32, 113
Mintz, I., 73, 112
Mitchell, H. D. Jr., 10, 107
Mitchell, J. E., 68, 112
Montague, A., 54, 112
Morris, L. A., 59, 73, 114
Morrison, J. K., 17, 112

Murray, E. J., 11, 19, 112

Nair, N. P., 70, 112
Nash, J. L., 23, 112
Nathan, P. E., 34, 113
Naylor, G. J., 60, 106
Nedelman, P. J., 98, 116
Nelson, W. M., 8, 112
Nichols, A. W., 43, 111
Norton, C. A., 8, 112

O'Brian, J. D., 66, 111
O'Connell, R. A., 66, 111
Olin, H. S., 8, 112
Oliver, L., 51, 112
Olson, E. J., 60, 112
Orgel, M., 25, 105
Orlinsky, D. E., 7, 112
Otteson, J. P., 37, 112

Padow, E., 9, 37, 112
Pappas, K., 70, 111
Parloff, M. B., 51, 54, 112
Pasamanick, B., 60, 112
Pasternack, C. H., 22, 113
Patterson, C. H., 12, 113
Paul, O. H., 4, 113
Pepitone-Rockwell, F., 5, 113
Pereira, J. A., 60, 113
Peterson, D. R., 17, 113
Phillips, D. R., 46, 113
Plotkin, R., 34, 89, 113
Pope, A., 39
Pritchard, D. A., 54, 113

Reppucci, N. D., 32, 106
Rice, D. E., 50, 113
Rice, I. K., 50, 113
Rickard, H. C., 36, 107
Rickels, K., 60, 113
Riscalla, L. M., 45, 113
Roach, J. L., 47, 113
Rodrigues, T., 66, 107
Rogers, C. R., 3, 11, 37, 113
Roll, S., 32, 53, 113
Rosenblatt, A., 54, 113
Rosenkrantz, P., 51, 106

Rosenthal, R., 10, 113
Ross, A. O., 31, 32, 34, 113
Roth, L. H., 96, 113
Routsonis, C., 70, 111
Ruesch, J., 1, 10, 113
Rutter, M., 33, 113
Ryle, A., 36, 113
Rynearson, R. R., 89, 113

Sandler, K. R., 60, 113
Santos, A. B., 69, 113
Saretsky, L., 52, 113
Sawin, L. G., 32, 109
Scarpetti, S. R., 60, 112
Schacht, T., 34, 113
Schaffer, K. F., 5, 51, 113
Schain, R. J., 34, 114
Scheff, T. J., 34, 114
Schimel, J. L., 11, 114
Schless, A. P., 60, 113
Schmidt, J. P., 53, 114
Schulman, J. L., 19, 20, 111
Schofield, W., 32, 37, 44, 114
Schweitzer, A., 56
Seagull, A. A., 54, 110
Seiden, R. H., 90, 108
Senay, E. C., 60, 106
Seterling, F. E., 70, 111
Shah, S., 90, 91, 114
Shakespeare, W., 56
Shapiro, A. K., 59, 73, 114
Shertzer, B., 1, 17, 114
Sheryle, J. W., 5, 105
Siassi, I., 33, 107
Sice, J., 73, 111
Sidel, R., 37, 114
Siegel, M., 87, 89, 94, 114
Simek-Downing, L., 10, 110
Slaikeu, K. A., 18, 109
Sloane, R. B., 12, 114
Slovenko, R., 89, 91, 96–99, 114
Smith, M. L., 51, 54, 114
Smith, S. R., 101, 112
Smymer, M. A., 47, 114
Sobel, D., 60, 114
Solomon, J. C., 70, 105
Solomon, K., 66, 107

Spensley, J., 4, 10, 114
Spiegel, S. B., 51, 114
Spiro, H. R., 33, 107
Spokane, A. R., 4, 111
Springer, K., 53, 108
Spruill, J., 94, 111
Standal, S. W., 27, 48, 99, 114
Staples, F. R., 12, 114
Stein, L. S., 62, 114
Steiner, G. L., 44, 114
Steinzor, B., 23, 114
Stockdale, S. L., 60, 115
Stokes, J., 51, 114
Stone, S. C., 1, 17, 114
Storandt, M., 45, 114
Strassberg, D. S., 10, 114
Strauss, J. S., 47, 65, 106, 115
Strupp, H., 3, 7, 8, 10–12, 16, 33, 115
Sue, D., 54, 115
Sue, D. W., 54, 115
Sviland, M. A. P., 46, 115
Szasz, T. S., 34, 99, 115

Tanney, M. F., 50, 51, 109, 115
Taratsidis, I., 70, 111
Thorne, F. T., 27, 115
Tolbert, E. L., 1–3, 7, 115
Toomer, J. E., 51, 115
Totman, R., 36, 115
Touliatos, J., 54, 115
True, R. H., 90, 108
Tuma, A. H., 72, 115

Vance, F. L., 4, 111
Vanden Bos, G. R., 11, 71, 72, 110
Van Hoose, W., 14, 115
Vogel, S. R., 51, 106

Wachtel, P. L., 12, 37, 115
Wallick, M. M., 46, 115
Wang, R. I., 60, 115
Ware, S., 47, 115
Warren, L. W., 37, 115
Waskow, I. E., 51, 54, 112
Waxler, N. E., 34, 115
Weinberg, J. R., 33, 115
Weinstein, H., 54, 110

Weintraub, W., 46, 115
Wenegrat, A., 4, 115
Werry, J. S., 34, 116
Whipple, K., 12, 114
Whitaker, L., 11, 72, 107
Wicas, E. A., 5, 105
Wilcox, E., 17, 116
Wilder, D. H., 52, 116
Williams, C. D., 45, 105
Wing, J. K., 60, 111
Wohl, J., 88, 99, 116

Wohlford, P., 45, 116
Wolfe, B. E., 51, 54, 112
Wollersheim, M. P., 24, 116

Yalom, I., 37, 116
Yorkston, N. J., 12, 114

Zaro, J. S., 98, 116
Zettle, R. D., 52, 116
Zwerling, I., 53, 111

Subject Index

Addiction, 19, 43, 60, 63, 73
Assessment, 34, 62, 80, 81, 83, 85
 and psychoactive drugs, 58, 61, 65,
  66, 68
 and psychotherapy, 26–29, 33, 38, 64

Behavior, 35, 36

Client,
 age, 39, 40, 44–48, 50
 expectations, 18–20, 24
 gender, 39, 40, 44, 48–52
 skin color, 39, 40, 44, 52–54
 strengths, 26, 34–37, 39
 YAVIS, 44
Communication, 7, 8, 83
Composure,
 client, 5, 6
 therapist, 3, 4, 42, 53, 62, 63
Confidentiality, 18, 25, 87, 89, 91–93,
  100, 101
Counseling, see Therapy
Counselor, see Therapist

Dangerousness, 96
Diagnosis, 26–33, 38, 53
DSM III, 26, 27, 30–33, 36
Duty to Warn, 89, 93–97

Empathy, 2–4, 42, 52, 62, 86

First meeting, 9, 14, 15–19, 24, 26, 27,
 29, 34

Heisenberg Uncertainty Principle, 28, 34
Homocide, 5, 93, 94

Limit-setting, 5

Patient, 35
 See also Client
Placebo, 36, 60, 61, 73, 74
Placebo effect, 12, 61, 73
Privilege, 87, 89, 90, 92
Psychoactive drugs,
 abuse, 57, 68, 69
 and therapy, 58, 61–66, 68
 cost-effectiveness, 58, 59, 61, 71–73
 defined, 56–57
 desired effects, 67–71
 side effects, 58, 59, 61, 63, 64,
  66–71, 73

Race, 40, 50, 53, 54
Record-Keeping, 25, 88, 89, 97–99
Referral, 4, 42, 52, 63, 74, 85

Suicide, 5, 68, 79–84

Tardive dyskenisia, 57, 67–69
Termination, 10, 15, 19–21, 24, 77,
 88, 103
Therapist,
 age, 39, 42
 bewilderment, 84–86
 characteristics, ix, 1, 2
 definition, 9

effectiveness, ix, 8, 11, 12, 21, 24, 43,
    48, 53, 56–58, 61, 64, 78, 79, 85, 97
encouragement, 8, 27, 35, 62, 63
flexibility, 11, 47, 54
gender, 39, 42
profession, 15–18, 100
skin color, 39, 40, 42
techniques, ix, 9, 11, 12
theoretical orientation, 1, 2, 7, 11
use of telephone, 15, 21, 25, 75–79, 82

    values, 80
Therapy,
    contract, 16, 24, 25, 46
    cost, 16, 20, 22, 23
    definitions, 2, 16
    discussion in, 6, 7
    goals, 9, 10, 25, 27, 98
    length of, 9, 10, 20, 21, 25, 30
Third party, 87–89, 91–93, 97, 99–101
Trust, 5, 87, 89, 90, 92, 94

About the Author

David Brenner received his undergraduate degree from Brown University and his Ph.D. in clinical psychology from Northwestern University in 1970. Dr. Brenner then went to Colgate University and was a faculty member in the Psychology Department and Associate University Counselor at Colgate's Counseling and Psychological Services. During his eleven years at Colgate, he provided psychotherapy and counseling for over 1,500 students, faculty, and staff and participated in the selection and training of graduate students in Colgate's Masters Degree Program in Counseling. Dr. Brenner is now in full-time private practice in Hamilton, New York and serves as a consultant to numerous organizations.

Pergamon General Psychology Series

Editors: Arnold P. Goldstein, Syracuse University
Leonard Krasner, SUNY, Stony Brook

Vol. 1. WOLPE—*The Practice of Behavior Therapy, Second Edition*
Vol. 2. MAGOON *et al*—*Mental Health Conselors at Work*
Vol. 3. McDANIEL—*Physical Disability and Human Behavior, Second Edition*
Vol. 4. KAPLAN *et al*—*The Structural Approach in Psychological Testing*
Vol. 5. LaFAUCI & RICHTER—*Team Teaching at the College Level*
Vol. 6. PEPINSKY *et al*—*People and Information*
Vol. 7. SIEGMAN & POPE—*Studies in Dyadic Communication*
Vol. 8. JOHNSON—*Existential Man: The Challenge of Psychotherapy*
Vol. 9. TAYLOR—*Climate for Creativity*
Vol. 10. RICKARD—*Behavioral Intervention in Human Problems*
Vol. 14. GOLDSTEIN—*Psychotherapeutic Attraction*
Vol. 15. HALPERN—*Survival: Black/White*
Vol. 16. SALZINGER & FELDMAN—*Studies in Verbal Behavior: An Empirical Approach*
Vol. 17. ADAMS & BOARDMAN—*Advances in Experimental Clinical Psychology*
Vol. 18. ZILLER—*The Social Self*
Vol. 19. LIBERMAN—*A Guide to Behavioral Analysis & Therapy*
Vol. 22. PEPINSKY & PATTON—*The Psychological Experiment: A Practical Accomplishment.*
Vol. 23. YOUNG—*New Sources of Self*
Vol. 24. WATSON—*Child Behavior Modification: A Manual for Teachers, Nurses, and Parents*
Vol. 25. NEWBOLD—*The Psychiatric Programming of People: Neo-Behavioral Orthomolecular Psychiatry*
Vol. 26. ROSSI—*Dreams and the Growth of Personality: Expanding Awareness in Psychotherapy*
Vol. 27. O'LEARY & O'LEARY—*Classroom Management: The Successful Use of Behavior Modification, Second Edition*
Vol. 28. FELDMAN—*College and Student: Selected Readings in the Social Psychology of Higher Education*
Vol. 29. ASHEM & POSER—*Adaptive Learning: Behavior Modification with Children*
Vol. 30. BURCK *et al*—*Counseling and Accountability: Methods and Critique*
Vol. 31. FREDERIKSEN *et al*—*Prediction of Organizational Behavior*
Vol. 32. CATTELL—*A New Morality from Science: Beyondism*
Vol. 33. WEINER—*Personality: The Human Potential*
Vol. 34. LIEBERT, NEALE & DAVIDSON—*The Early Window: Effects of Television on Children and Youth*
Vol. 35. COHEN *et al*—*Psych City: A Simulated Community*
Vol. 36. GRAZIANO—*Child Without Tomorrow*
Vol. 37. MORRIS—*Perspectives in Abnormal Behavior*

Vol. 38.   BALLER—*Bed Wetting: Origins and Treatment*
Vol. 40.   KAHN, CAMERON, & GIFFEN—*Psychological Methods in Evaluation and Counseling*
Vol. 41.   SEGALL—*Human Behavior and Public Policy: A Political Psychology*
Vol. 42.   FAIRWEATHER et al—*Creating Change in Mental Health Organizations*
Vol. 43.   KATZ & ZLUTNICK—*Behavior Therapy and Health Care: Principles and Applications*
Vol. 44.   EVANS & CLAIBORN—*Mental Health Issues and the Urban Poor*
Vol. 45.   HILLNER—*Psychology of Learning: A Conceptual Approach*
Vol. 46.   BARBER, SPANOS & CHAVES—*Hypnosis, Imagination and Human Potentialities*
Vol. 47.   POPE—*The Mental Health Interview*
Vol. 48.   PELTON—*The Psychology of Nonviolence*
Vol. 49.   COLBY—*Artificial Paranoia—A Computer Simulation of Paranoid Processes*
Vol. 50.   GELFAND & HARTMANN—*Child Behavior Analysis and Therapy*
Vol. 51.   WOLPE—*Theme and Variations: A Behavior Therapy Casebook*
Vol. 52.   KANFER & GOLDSTEIN—*Helping People Change: A Textbook of Methods, Second Edition*
Vol. 53.   DANZIGER—*Interpersonal Communication*
Vol. 54.   KATZ—*Towards the Elimination of Racism*
Vol. 55.   GOLDSTEIN & STEIN—*Prescriptive Psychotherapies*
Vol. 56.   HERSEN & BARLOW—*Single-Case Experimental Designs: Strategies for Studying Behavior Changes*
Vol. 57.   MONAHAN—*Community Mental Health and the Criminal Justice System*
Vol. 58.   WAHLER, HOUSE & STAMBAUGH—*Ecological Assessment of Child Behavior: A Clinical Package for Home, School, and Institutional Settings*
Vol. 59.   MAGARO—*The Construction of Madness—Emerging Conceptions and Interventions into the Psychotic Process*
Vol. 60.   MILLER—*Behavioral Treatments of Alcoholism*
Vol. 61.   FOREYT—*Behavioral Treatments of Obesity*
Vol. 62.   WANDERSMAN, POPPEN & RICKS—*Humanism and Behaviorism: Dialogue and Growth*
Vol. 63.   NIETZEL, WINETT, MACDONALD & DAVIDSON—*Behavioral Approaches to Community Psychology*
Vol. 64.   FISHER & GOCHROS—*Handbook of Behavior Therapy with Sexual Problems. Vol. I: General Procedures. Vol. II: Approaches to Specific Problems*
Vol. 65.   HERSEN & BELLACK—*Behavioral Assessment: A Practical Handbook, Second Edition*
Vol. 66.   LEFKOWITZ, ERON, WALDER & HUESMANN—*Growing Up To Be Violent: A Longitudinal Study of the Development of Aggression*
Vol. 67.   BARBER—*Pitfalls in Human Research: Ten Pivotal Points*
Vol. 68.   SILVERMAN—*The Human Subject in the Psychological Laboratory*

Vol. 69. FAIRWEATHER & TORNATZKY—*Experimental Methods for Social Policy Research*
Vol. 70. GURMAN & RAZIN—*Effective Psychotherapy: A Handbook of Research*
Vol. 71. MOSES & BYHAM—*Applying the Assessment Center Method*
Vol. 72. GOLDSTEIN—*Prescriptions for Child Mental Health and Education*
Vol. 73. KEAT—*Multimodal Therapy with Children*
Vol. 74. SHERMAN—*Personality: Inquiry & Application*
Vol. 75. GATCHEL & PRICE—*Clinical Applications of Biofeedback: Appraisal and Status*
Vol. 76. CATALANO—*Health, Behavior and the Community: An Ecological Perspective*
Vol. 77. NIETZEL—*Crime and Its Modification: A Social Learning Perspective*
Vol. 78. GOLDSTEIN, HOYER & MONTI—*Police and the Elderly*
Vol. 79. MIRON & GOLDSTEIN—*Hostage*
Vol. 80. GOLDSTEIN *et al*—Police Crisis Intervention
Vol. 81. UPPER & CAUTELA—*Covert Conditioning*
Vol. 82. MORELL—*Program Evaluation in Social Research*
Vol. 83. TEGER—*Too Much Invested to Quit*
Vol. 84. MONJAN & GASSNER—*Critical Issues in Competency-Based Education*
Vol. 85. KRASNER—*Environmental Design and Human Behavior: A Psychology of the Individual in Society*
Vol. 86. TAMIR—*Communication and the Aging Process: Interaction Throughout the Life Cycle*
Vol. 87. WEBSTER, KONSTANTAREAS, OXMAN & MACK—*Autism: New Directions in Research and Education*
Vol. 88. TRIESCHMANN—*Spinal Cord Injuries*

Vol. 89. CARTLEDGE & MILBURN—*Teaching Social Skills to Children: Innovative Approaches*
Vol. 90. SARBIN & MANCUSO—*Schizophrenia — Medical Diagnosis or Moral Verdict?*
Vol. 91. RATHJEN & FOREYT—*Social Competence: Interventions for Children and Adults*
Vol. 92. VAN DE RIET, KORB & GORRELL—*Gestalt Therapy: An Introduction*
Vol. 93. MARSELLA & PEDERSEN—*Cross-Cultural Counseling and Psychotherapy*
Vol. 94. BRISLIN—*Cross-Cultural Encounters: Face-to-Face Interaction*
Vol. 95. SCHWARTZ & JOHNSON—*Psychopathology of Childhood: A Clinical-Experimental Approach*
Vol. 96. HEILBRUN—*Human Sex-Role Behavior*
Vol. 97. DAVIDSON, KOCH, LEWIS & WRESINSKI—*Evaluation Strategies in Criminal Justice*

Vol. 98. GOLDSTEIN, CARR, DAVIDSON, WEHR—*In Response to Aggression: Methods of Control and Prosocial Alternatives*
Vol. 99. GOLDSTEIN — *Psychological Skill Training: The Structured Learning Technique*
Vol. 100. WALKER — *Clinical Practice of Psychology: A Guide for Mental Health Professionals*
Vol. 101. ANCHIN & KIESLER — *Handbook of Interpersonal Psychotherapy*
Vol. 102. GELLER, WINETT, EVERETT — *Preserving the Environment: New Strategies for Behavior Change*
Vol. 103. JENKINS — *The Psychology of the Afro-American: A Humanistic Approach*
Vol. 104. APTER — *Troubled Children/Troubled Systems*
Vol. 105. BRENNER — *The Effective Psychotherapist: Conclusions from Practice and Research*
Vol. 106. KAROLY & KANFER — *Self-Management and Behavior Change: From Theory to Practice*
Vol. 107. O'BRIEN, DICKINSON, ROSOW — *Industrial Behavior Modification: A Management Handbook*